quilting on the go... English Paper Piecing

SHARON BURGESS

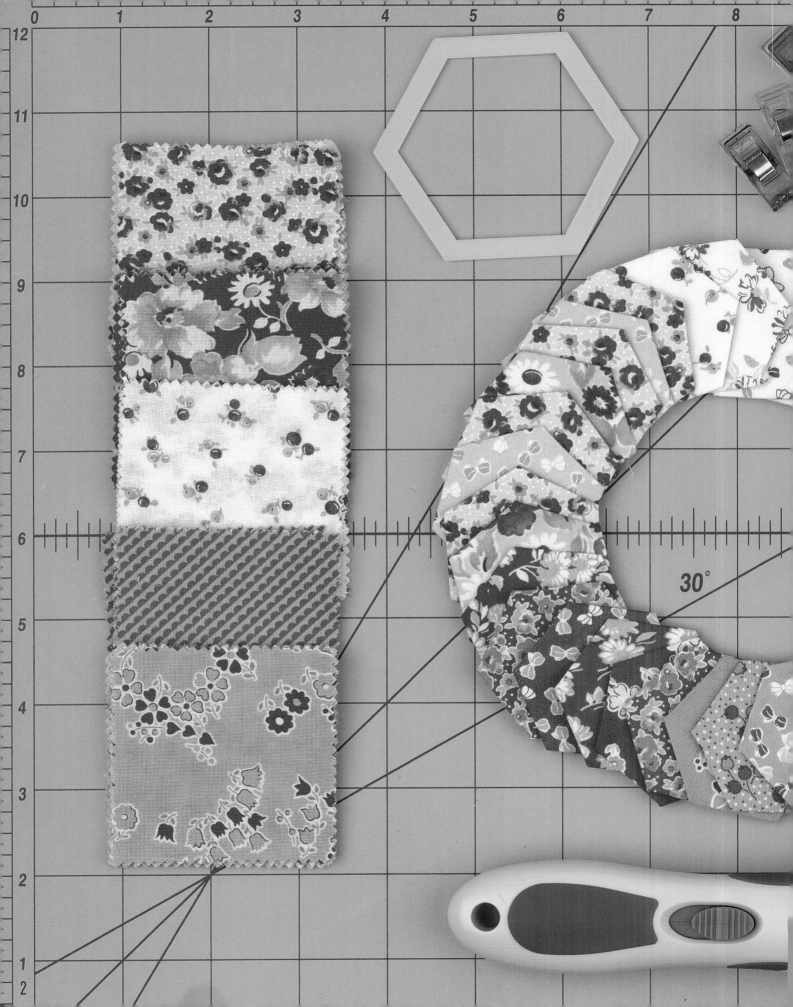

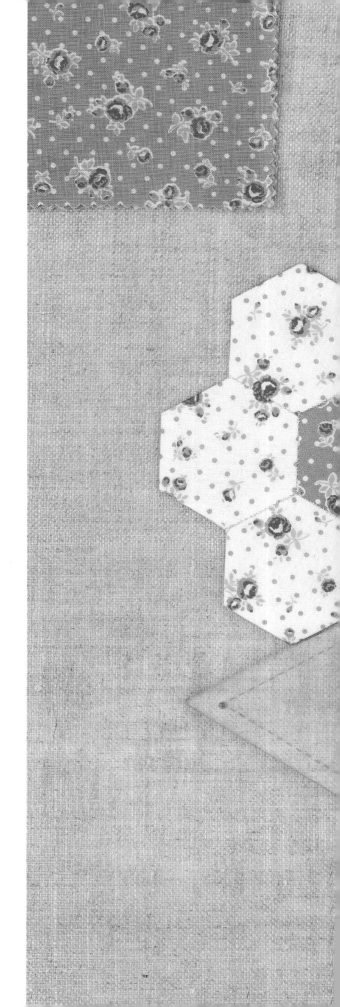

Tuva Publishing

www.tuvapublishing.com

Address Merkez Mah. Cavusbasi Cad. No:71
Cekmekoy - Istanbul 34782 / Turkey
Tel: +9 0216 642 62 62

Quilting on the Go
English Paper Piecing

First Print 2017 / June

All Global Copyrights Belong To
Tuva Tekstil ve Yayıncılık Ltd.

Content Quilting

Editor in Chief Ayhan DEMİRPEHLİVAN
Project Editor Kader DEMİRPEHLİVAN
Designer Sharon BURGESS
Technical Editors Leyla ARAS, Büşra ESER
Proof Reading Samantha RICHTER, Glenn DUNCAN
Graphic Designers Ömer ALP, Abdullah BAYRAKÇI
Assistant Zilal ÖNEL
Photograph Tuva Publishing, Sharon BURGESS
Illustrations Murat Tanhu YILMAZ

ISBN 978-605-9192-22-4

Printing House
Bilnet Matbaacılık ve Yayıncılık A.Ş.

 TuvaYayincilik TuvaPublishing
 TuvaYayincilik TuvaPublishing

CONTENTS

TECHNIQUES

PROJECTS

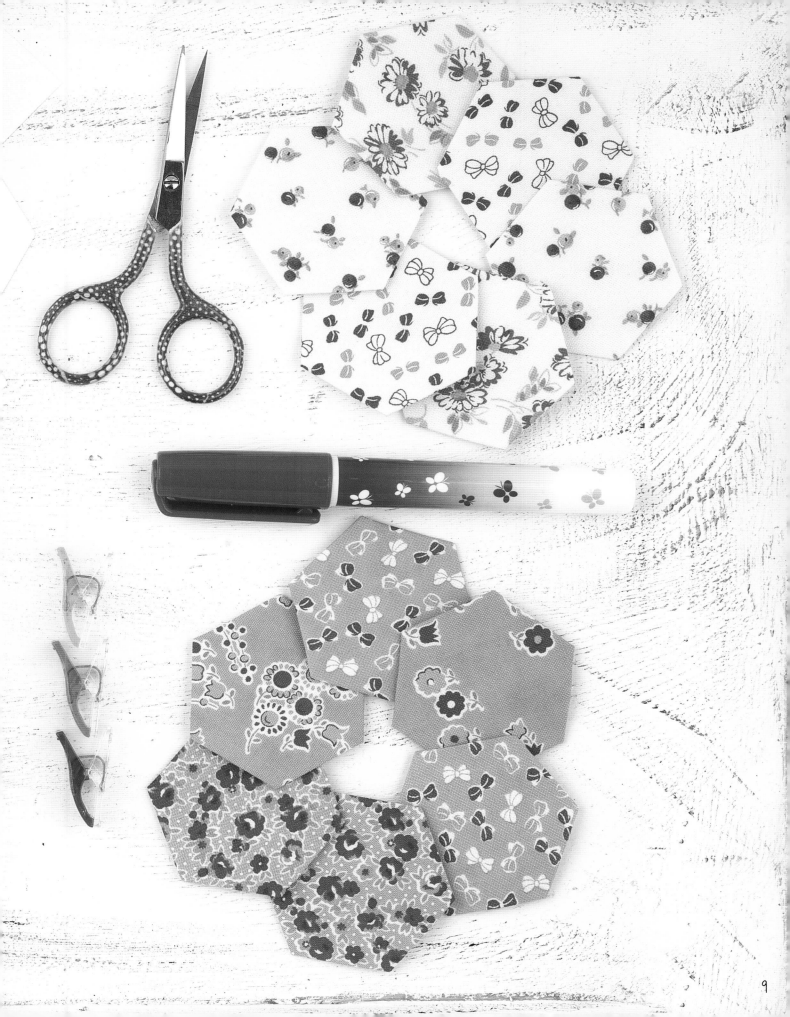

INTRODUCTION

I was born in the United Kingdom and at a young age came to Australia with my family. My dad was a mechanic by trade but of an evening I remember him always dragging the dining table into the lounge room so we would all be together as a family unit in the one room and he would paint. Sadly, he passed way too young and never got to share his talents with me in person. My mother was always at the sewing machine sewing clothing for us as children and I have vivid memories of my mum sewing a wedding dress for a family friend, but it was not until I had my own children that I thought about my own creative journey.

An urgent need for another hobby lead me to borrowing my mother's sewing machine. I had always had the desire to make a quilt so whilst I had my mums machine I went into my local quilt shop and signed up for a beginner's class. This was back in 2009 and now there are not many days that don't somehow involve my needle and thread meeting fabric in some way.

It was not long into my sewing journey that I discovered English Paper Piecing. I was hooked. My passion for English Paper Piecing grew stronger and my true love for the craft and fussy cutting really took off when I started making my "La Passacaglia Quilt" back in July 2014. I was making this quilt before it became the 'fashionable' quilt to make. The ability to take a fabric and cut it in such a way that creates new patterns, and to incorporate that into an existing pattern allows me to truly make something that is my own and unique to me.

I now teach the technique of English Paper Piecing to both new and experienced students. I enjoy watching them embrace the process and potentially make heirlooms for their families to love and cherish for the years to come.

I love to be able to take an English Paper Pieced panel that I have made and to incorporate it into another sewn project, and I share the technique I use within this book. You can make any project truly your own, and you are only limited by your imagination.

My dream for this book is that, if you have never English Paper Pieced before, that you pick up your needle and thread and not be scared to give it a go. Learn to enjoy the process and joy that can come from stitching something with your own hands. If you are experienced, I hope that you are inspired by the projects within this book, and venture into the journey of fabric selection and create one of my projects in such a way that makes it your own.

I have one rule for myself and one word of advice for you.

"Create what you love".

Happy stitching,

Sharon

PROJECT GALLERY

32

44

48

54

38

72

66

76

80

84

90

96

102

108

114

118

WHAT IS ENGLISH PAPER PIECING?

Put simply, English Paper Piecing (commonly referred to as EPP) is a technique used for making quilts by hand where your fabric is basted over a paper template, then the shapes are sewn together to form the quilt or project.

English Paper Piecing is sometimes also known as "Mosaic Patchwork" and when English Paper Piecing is spoken of, hexagon quilts usually come to mind. The hexagon shape has been hugely popular over the centuries and is the shape that has been predominantly used from as far back as the 1700s.

Popular through Europe and specifically England, it became exceptionally fashionable in the United States of America towards late 18th Century. when anything English was considered highly fashionable.

One of the most popular and most recognizable English Paper Piecing patterns was and still is, the "Grandmother's Flower Garden". It is based around seven simple hexagons sewn together to form a flower shape. It could be used to create a simple block, or with more sewn together, it could form an entire quilt. With the onset of the Great Depression in the USA in the 1930s, this quilt pattern could easily be created with leftover fabric scraps, with the papers being recycled from documents and books.

"Celestial Star" can be found on page 54

PAPERS AND TEMPLATES

Paper shapes are the backbone of English Paper Piecing projects, and a wide variety of pre-cut paper pieces can be purchased to create almost anything. As the pre-cut paper pieces are professionally die-cut, accuracy is assured. This is critical for EPP.

You can cut your own template shapes, but care needs to be taken to ensure accuracy.

There are some shapes used in these patterns that are not readily available. You will see these shapes marked with an * on them – see Templates (pages 122-126).

For shapes that are not available in your local quilt shop, you will need to transfer the shape onto cardstock/thick paper (I use a 160gsm cardstock) and then cut them yourself. Alternatively, check my website for available kits.

Acrylic templates are used to assist you in cutting and tracing the required shape onto your fabric. They come complete with a seam allowance for basting to your paper pieces. They are clear to allow you to see what you are cutting, essential when fussy cutting. They can be commonly purchased with a ¼" or ⅜" seam allowance.

TIP: Making Your Own Template
Lay a paper shape onto some template plastic and carefully, with a rotary cutter and an add-a-quarter ruler cut the template plastic ¼" bigger than your shape. A plastic template is easier to mark reference points for fussy cutting with a pencil and the marks simply erase off.

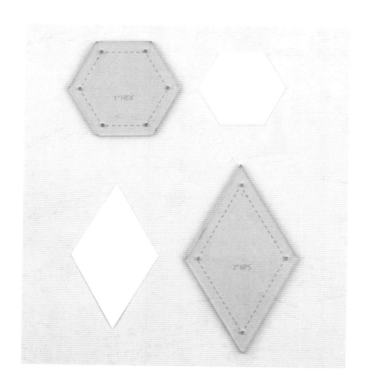

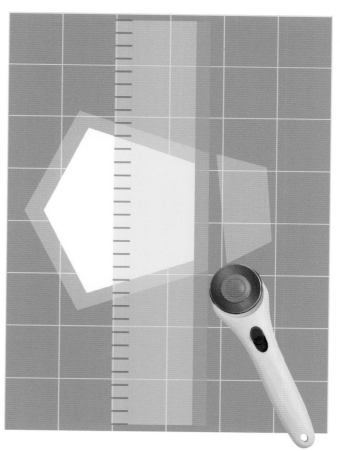

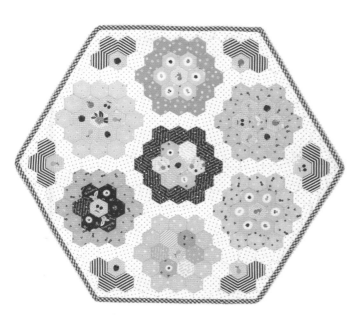

"Flower Garden Mini Quilt"
can be found on page 44

15

MY ESSENTIAL ENGLISH PAPER PIECING TOOLS

Having the right tools on hand will make your English Paper Piecing journey a more enjoyable one. All the items I have here can be found in your local patchwork shop or easily online.

▶ Size 11 Milliner's needles (also known as straw needles)
▶ Thread
▶ Glue pen and refills
▶ Rotary cutters - both 60mm and 28mm
▶ Scissors
▶ Rotating cutting mat
▶ Cutting mat
▶ Sandpaper board
▶ Quilting clips

▶ Pencil
▶ Appliqué glue
▶ Patchwork ruler
▶ Fussy Cutting Mirror
▶ Add-a-quarter-ruler
▶ Seam ripper
▶ ¼" masking tape
▶ 'Flatter' by SOAK

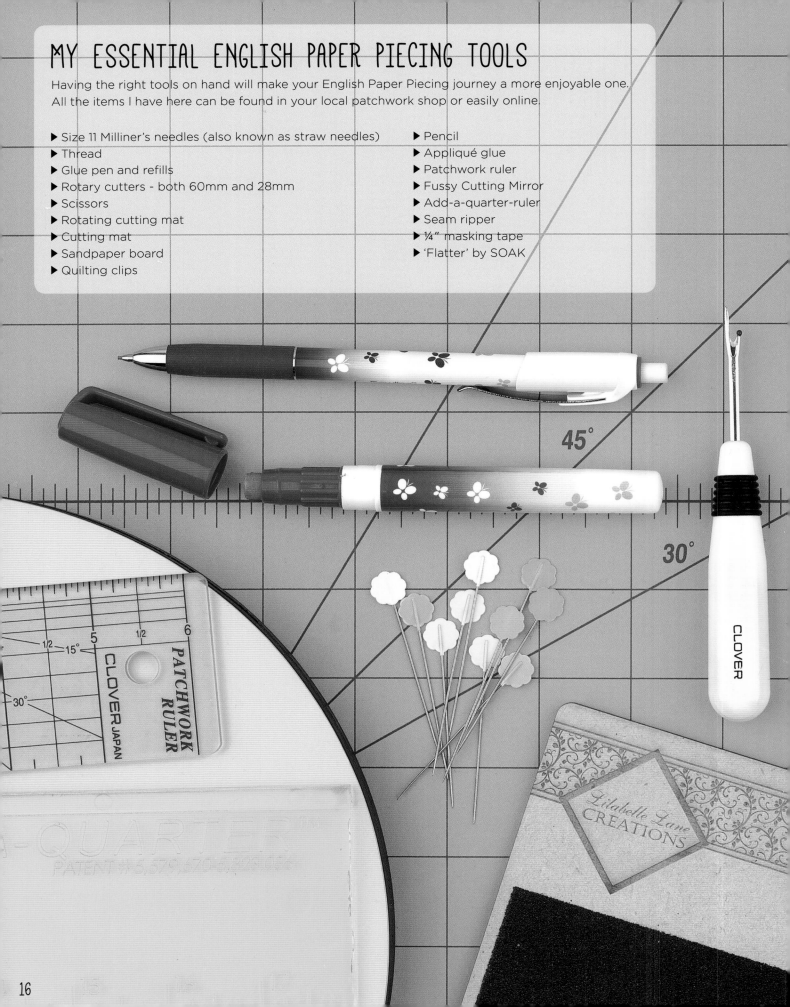

Fussy Cutting Mirror

Lilabelle Lane CREATIONS

so create
what YOU love

Sharon

CLOVER CUTTING MAT

17

NEEDLES

Everyone has their favorite. Mine are the size 11 Milliner's needles. The finer your needle and thread, the easier it is to sew beautiful, invisible stitches. Teaming the right needle and thread is the key to achieving your best possible work.

THREAD

I only use Superior Bottom Line thread 60wt for my English Paper Piecing. This is a polyester thread. Traditionally, if you are working with cotton fabric, you would use a cotton thread but with English Paper Piecing every time you make a stitch your thread is rubbing against the paper template, and when using a cotton thread it can fray and snap. The polyester thread does not. So, for the purpose of English Paper Piecing I love my Superior Bottom Line thread. It is available in doughnuts which gives you a great assortment of colors (it is also great for appliqué), or you can also get a small collection of individual Superbobs in a variety of neutral and commonly used colors, which are great for the stitcher on the move, or alternatively on the spool which holds 1420 yards.

GLUE PEN

Glue pens are used to stick your fabric to your paper templates and makes for a speedy process. They are a great alternative to thread basting.

TIP: In a warmer climate you can store your glue pen and refills in a refrigerator in an airtight container or place your glue pen and refills in the refrigerator for half an hour before use to firm up the glue. This will help prevent you from using to much glue on your papers.

ROTARY CUTTERS AND SCISSORS

When cutting my shapes from fabric, I use both my rotary cutters and fabric shears. You will also need a nice, comfortable pair of small embroidery scissors for cutting your thread.

ROTATING CUTTING MAT / CUTTING MAT

A rotating cutting mat is great when it comes to cutting individual pieces of fabric, as you are moving the cutting surface not your fabric and template. It is a great tool to help you achieve nice smooth curved surfaces when basting your papers.

SANDPAPER BOARD

A sandpaper board helps to grip your fabric and eliminates movement when you are tracing your template shape onto your fabric with your pencil.

QUILTING CLIPS

These are great to hold your pieces together as you stitch. They reduce strain on your hand from holding your pieces too tight, and are also useful for holding groups of prepared pieces together for when you are stitching on the go. You can also use them to hold your binding in place/folded over whilst you stitch down your binding.

PENCIL

I use a re-fillable clutch pencil.

APPLIQUÉ GLUE

This eliminates the need for pins when positioning shapes to be appliquéd to another piece of fabric. It's also great for allowing you to prepare your hand work to take with you on the go.

PATCHWORK RULER

Various sizes are handy to help with your rotary cutting of fabric.

FUSSY CUTTING MIRROR

With the investment of a Fussy Cutting mirror, you will be able to see all of your options within your pattern repeats and how you can use them to create new and exciting layouts.

ADD-A-QUARTER RULER

This is a good tool to help when making your own templates and anywhere you need to add a ¼" seam allowance.

SEAM RIPPER

A nice sharp seam ripper is essential to help with any reverse sewing.

¼" MASKING TAPE

I use my ¼" masking tape to help keep my hand quilting lines straight. Line it up along where you want to hand quilt and follow the edge so that your hand quilting lines stay nice and straight.

FLATTER BY SOAK

I prefer to use Flatter by SOAK on all my sewing. It is a starch-free smoothing agent that leaves my sewing 'sleek, soft and static free'.

HOW ARE THE SHAPES MEASURED?

Pre-cut paper pieces are sold in various sizes to suit your design needs. Geometric shapes are measured by measuring one of the equal sides. This hexagon below is the 1" size.

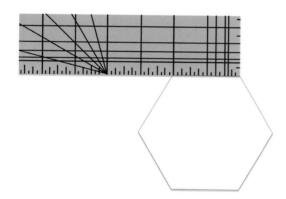

Curved paper pieces are measured across the diameter.

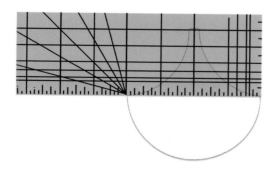

And some other examples...

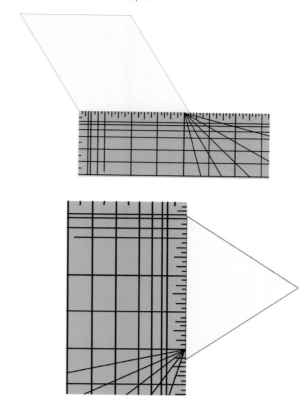

A QUICK NOTE ON FABRIC REQUIREMENTS

Because of the nature of many projects within my book and the fussy cutting, exact fabric requirements can not be given for the EPP components, so please, when you are selecting your fabrics, take this into consideration. Thank you.

TECHNIQUES

GETTING STARTED

Glue basting is a simple and time-effective way to prepare your papers and fabrics for stitching.

HOW TO GLUE YOUR PAPERS

1 Lay your fabrics right side down, place your paper on top and center.

2 Holding your glue pen on an angle, just like you hold a pen, glide it across the paper slightly away from the edge. This will come with practice. We do this so it makes it easy to guide your needle through your fabric and not also through dried glue.

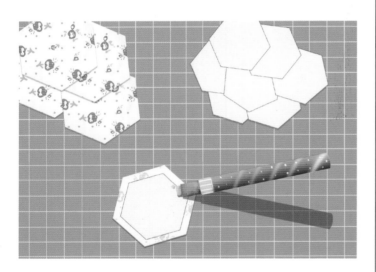

3 Fold over the fabric and press down. Continue to the next side and repeat. Ensure that your points are nice and sharp. Repeat for all the sides of your shape.

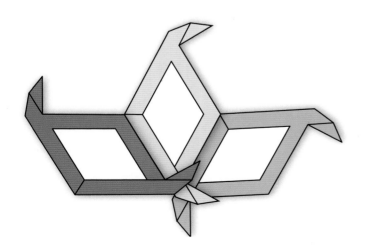

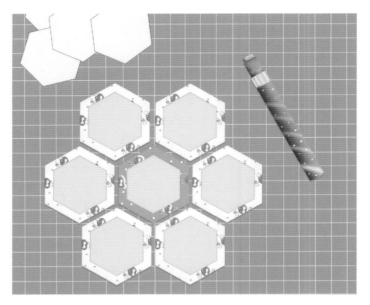

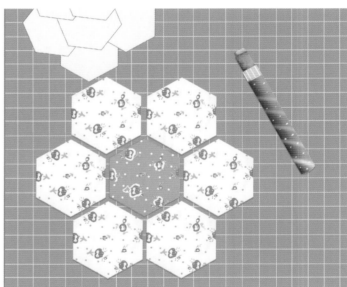

TIP: It is a good habit to always glue your papers in the same direction regardless of shape. This helps when you are using diamonds/stars and triangles as the tails will all sit the same way at the back and creates neater, flatter work.

You can begin to remove the papers once they are all surrounded by more papers / blocks. As a piece of work grows you only need the outer most edge to have papers left in. By removing your papers, your work will be lighter and easier to handle. To remove your papers gently peel back the fabric and your papers should just peel out. If you are having trouble removing your papers it may be because you have used too much glue. If this is the case dampen the fabric to soften the glue or press lightly with a steam iron to soften and then remove your papers. Over time you will learn to be light-handed with the glue.

PREPARING PAPERS WITH CURVES

When preparing Clamshells, you only need to glue baste the top curve.

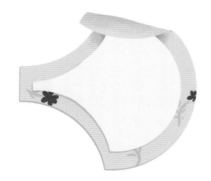

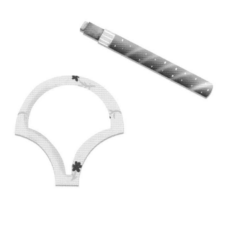

1 Lay your fabric right side down on a rotating mat and place your paper on top, centering it. Holding your glue pen on an angle, glide it across the curve of the paper slightly away from the edge.

2 Start at one side of your curve and fold the fabric over, forming little pleats as you go. The pleats will be at the back of your shape and the front should be nice and smooth.

If you do this step on a rotating mat you can turn your shape by turning the rotating mat without moving the fabric and paper, thus creating a smoother curve.

When basting flower petals, you would continue to baste around the entire shape.

JOINING THE PIECES – STRAIGHT EDGED SHAPES

1 Thread your needle with a coordinating thread and tie a knot in one end.

2 Place two shapes right side together. Slide your needle up under the fabric at the start point and pull through to bury your thread.

3 At the very edge of your work slide the needle through both pieces of fabric, ensuring that you only catch a couple of threads and not the paper, and do your first stitch.

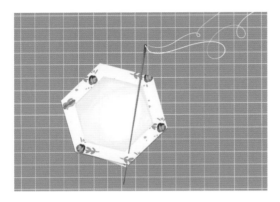

4 Secure your stitch on top of where you have just taken your first stitch. I secure my stitches by leaving a small loop in my thread and wrapping the needle around twice and pulling through.

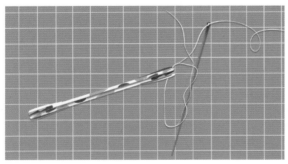

5 Using a Whip stitch (refer to hand stitches in the Techniques section), stitch along the edge of your shape making small stitches, securing your thread at the end. Remember with your Whip stitch to stitch the most direct path i.e. directly across the two pieces, not on an angle.

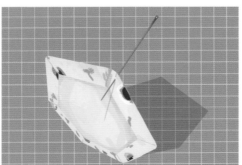

6 Open and then proceed to join in your next piece. There is no right or wrong way in which order to sew hexagons together.

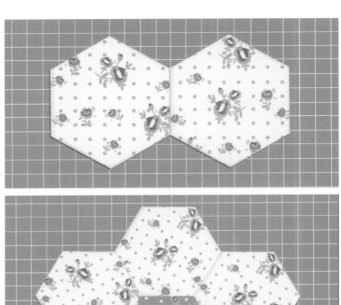

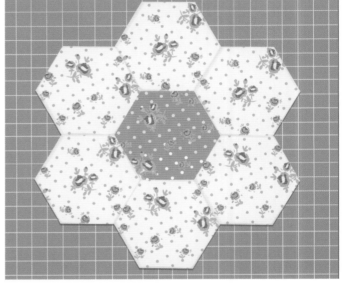

With 6 Pointed Diamonds, sew two sections of three and then sew those two sections together, from one side right through the middle to the other side. This stops any holes from forming at the meeting point of all your points.

If sewing an 8 or 10 pointed star, then the process is the same - two halves of 4 or 5 and then sew the two halves together.

As you are joining your pieces, do not to sew in the little tails. Fold them out of the way as you sew. These will sit nicely behind your work when you have finished.

As you sew your pieces together you may find it necessary to fold some papers. These can be ironed later ready for re-use.

Once you have finished a section, give it a quick press with an iron before removing any papers. This helps give your joins a nice neat finish.

JOINING THE PIECES - CLAMSHELLS

Joining clamshells is a little different from the normal EPP process. Prepare your clamshell papers and fabric as per the Glue Basting Curves instructions. Lay your prepared clamshells out in a pleasing manner. Clamshells are first joined together in rows and then appliquéd together.

To join your rows:

1 Thread your needle with a coordinating thread and tie a knot in one end.

2 Face two Clamshells right sides together and "kiss the points" by aligning the points at the start of the curve.

3 Make your first stitch right at the position where the papers align.

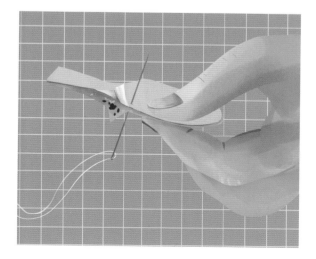

4 Make a couple of stitches on top of each other and then secure your stitch. Cut your thread and repeat the process for your desired number of clamshells. Repeat for the required number of rows.

5 To begin to sew your rows together, get a piece of fabric a little longer than the panel you plan on making.

6 Press a fold line approximately 1" along the bottom with your iron.

7 Using your appliqué glue, place three small dots of glue on the wrong side of the fabric of each clamshell. Flip over and align the top curve of the clamshell on the fold line. Allow the glue to dry naturally. Alternatively, move to your ironing board so that you can give everything a quick iron once glued into position to help set the glue quicker.

8 Appliqué your clamshells onto the fabric. Stitch around to each point where you "kissed your points" and then go up and over your next curve and continue until the row is completed - see "Blind stitch" in the Techniques section.

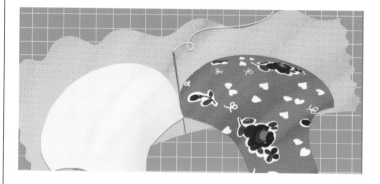

9 To remove your papers, you need to gently pull them out in a curved motion in line with the curve of the clamshell.

STRIP CUTTING YOUR FABRIC

If you are not fussy cutting your fabric you can strip cut.

1 Measure the height of your template against your ruler. Cut your fabric strips to this width.

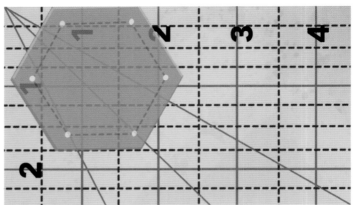

10 Line up your next prepared row, on your ironing board and apply three dots of appliqué glue to the wrong side of each clamshell.

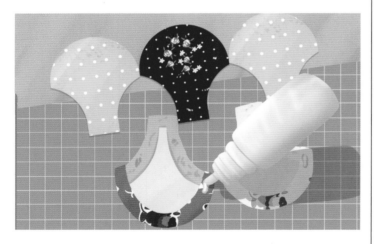

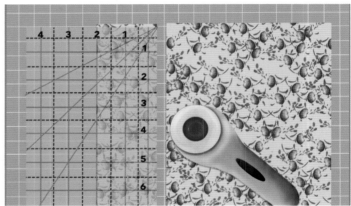

2 Position your perspex template on your fabric and cut with your rotary cutter, continuing along the strip of fabric. You can layer a few strips on top of each other to make multiple cuts and save you time. This works best with a sharp blade in your rotary cutter.

11 Flip over onto your previous row. This time you are aligning the top middle of the curve to the spot where you "kissed your points". Appliqué this row on as per step 8.

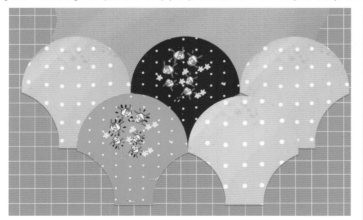

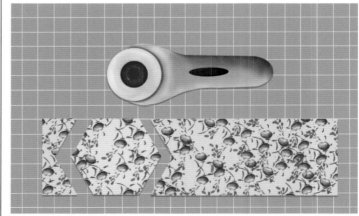

FUSSY CUTTING

There are two types of fussy cutting. The first and easiest is where you are fussy cutting out a specific part of the fabric to highlight it. It is simple yet effective at showcasing a particular part of a print.

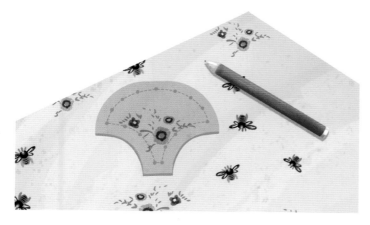

To achieve this, place your template over the fabric. Ensure that the part of the print on the fabric you are wanting to highlight is within the etched line of your template (not in the seam allowance section). Carefully cut with a rotary cutter or draw a line around the shape and use scissors to cut.

The second is where you are looking to make more of a kaleidoscope effect by cutting the same repeat of fabric multiple times. This works well with diamonds and stars and some lovely results can also be achieved with hexagons. When shopping for fabric to fussy cut try to look for fabrics with symmetrical designs and close repeats as these work best and can offer less wastage.

A fussy cutting mirror is a great tool for seeing all your fussy cutting options.

1 Place your mirror on your fabric, with your template or fussy cutting viewers in the center and slide it around. Explore all your fussy cutting options. Look for secondary patterns that can also form.

2 Once you have picked your 'fussy cut', remove your mirror and have a closer look at your fabric. Look for reference points to help with the accuracy in being able to consistently baste your papers in the same spot. In this example I am looking at the little pink dot at the bottom. I will be able to consistently line the points of my diamonds (the papers) on it when basting. At the top I know that I will be able to line the top point of the paper to the center of the print. Sometimes moving your chosen cut over ever so slightly to allow for a reference point to lay your paper on will be a big help with accuracy and lining up the fabric repeats for a more seamless finish once sewn together.

Check you have enough repeats on your fabric before continuing.

3 Place your fabric right side down on your sandpaper board, find your reference points again and with a pencil, trace your desired number of repeats.

TIP: I always draw on the wrong side of my fabric just in case I make a mistake in placement. It is much easier to retrace rather than having to worry about removing the pencil lines from the right side of the fabric.

4 With a sharp pair of pointed scissors, cut your shapes out along your drawn line. You can use a rotary cutter to do this but my preferred method is with scissors. I have greater control and I am not snipping into the remaining fabric like you do with a rotary cutter. This means that I potentially have more fabric available to fussy cut later with no little cuts into it.

5 Line your papers up with your reference points and baste. - (see Techniques section – Glue Basting).

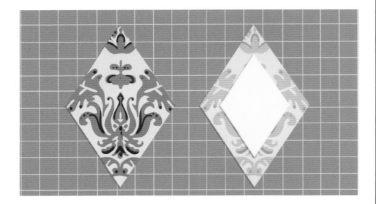

6 You are ready to sew, but before you do, flip them around and see if you created another pattern. You might like it more.

INCLUDING EPP IN ANY PROJECT

Incorporating an English Paper Pieced panel into any craft project is a fun way to make something that little more special and it is not hard to do. It can be as simple as substituting an EPP panel for a bag pocket or a dress bodice. This will require you to trim your panel to the correct size. Before trimming, mark the cutting line on the EPP panel with a water erasable fabric pen and then take the panel to your sewing machine. With a shorter stitch, sew approximately 1/8" inside the cut line all around. I like to go around mine twice. This will help your hand stitching from unravelling once the panel is cut to size.

If you have pieced a bigger panel of work and you want to add a border, simply remove all the papers from your work and press the seam allowance out. This is another reason not to sew in your little tails as they will sit nice and flat once unfolded and pressed out.

Again, sew around your panel ⅛" inside the cut line. On this example I am cutting ¼" out from the points.

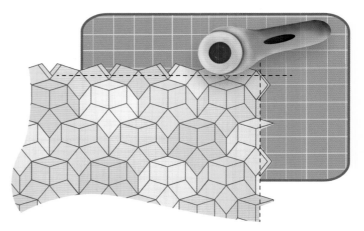

With larger EPP panels or quilts that you are trimming, take care to support the panel and not let any weight hang, as this can distort the panel.

HAND STITCHES

WHIP STITCH

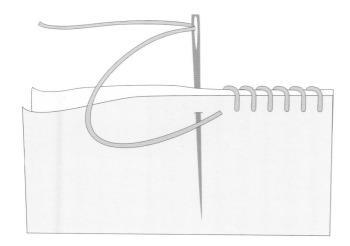

Knot one end of your single thread. Push your needle and thread through both layers of fabric, only taking a few threads from both. Take the needle to the back and bring it back through both layers again. Ensure that your stitches are taking the shortest path by coming straight through both fabrics, not on an angle.

RUNNING STITCH

Running stitch would be one of the commonly used embroidery stitches. Knot the end of your thread and bring your needle up at 1, down at 2, up at 3 and down at 4. With this stitch you need to try and keep your stitches at regular intervals and keep an even tension to avoid your stitches from puckering. I also like use a ¼" quilter's masking tape to help keep the lines straight on my work.

BLIND STITCH

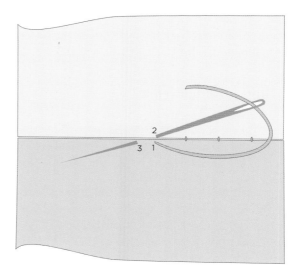

The most commonly used stitch for appliquéing onto a background.

Knot the end of a single thread and bring your needle up through the underneath of your background fabric barley piercing the edge of the piece you are appliquéing. Place the needle back into the background fabric directly opposite where you came out and bring the needle back up through all the fabrics about ¹⁄₁₆" on from the last stitch. Continue all the way around your appliqué piece. Take the needle and thread to the back of your work and knot to finish.

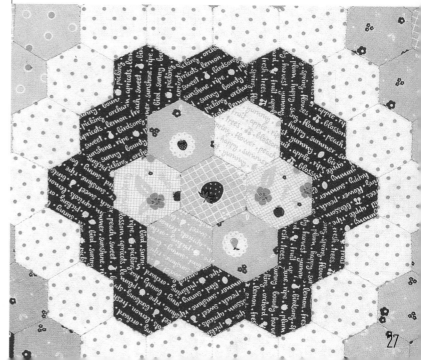

QUILTING

When you have finished piecing your quilt top, pillow top, table runner top or even your notebook cover it is time to quilt your project. If you are choosing to quilt the project yourself, you will need to make a quilt sandwich. If you are sending your item out to be professionally quilted, then your quilter will take care of this step.

MAKING A QUILT SANDWICH

A quilt sandwich is made from three layers. Your backing fabric, batting/parlan, and your top. For smaller projects I like to use parlan (a lightweight fusible wadding).

To make your sandwich you need to place your backing fabric right side down, layer your batting on your backing, and then place your top right side up on top of all the layers. You need to baste your layers together with either a basting spray (follow the instruction on the label) or curved basting pins. If using basting pins, start in the center of your piece and work out, ensuring that you have no wrinkles or pleats, especially on the back.

When I use parlan, I fuse it to the back of my top and then pin-baste the backing fabric to the parlan/top.

The next step is to sew the three layers together.

HAND QUILTING

Hand quilting adds a special touch to any project. It can take a little longer to finish your project but the effect is worth it when it is all done. Basically hand quilting is simply a running stitch done by hand. I don't use hand quilting nearly enough but when I do I love how it can highlight a section. I use 2 or 3 strands of coordinating DMC embroidery floss for smaller projects or DMC Perle cotton No 8 for larger projects.

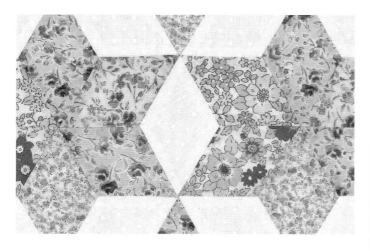

STRAIGHT LINE QUILTING

This is possibly one of the simplest forms of quilting to be achieved on a domestic sewing machine with a walking foot. You can do vertical, horizontal or even diagonal lines. Another favourite of mine is "in the ditch", which is simply sewing in the seam of two adjoining pieces. I like to team this up with some hand quilting.

FREE MOTION QUILTING

Free motion quilting is when you drop your feed dogs on your domestic machine, and with an open toe or darning foot, quilt your own design. Most common would be a stipple design where you meander around your quilt top and keep the space at approx. 1". You can also do feathers, leaves, pebbles and spiral to name just a few.

PROFESSIONAL LONG ARM QUILTING

I love the professional look and the texture that long arm quilting can give to your work. I send all my larger items out to be professionally quilted. A long arm quilter can offer an edge-to-edge design or you can work together on a custom design to make your quilt shine on a whole new level.

BINDING

To make your binding join your strips end to end by facing the fabric right sides together at a right angle to each other. Draw a 45 degree line and sew along this line with your machine. Trim ¼" away from the sewn line.

Press your seam open. Repeat to make the required amount of binding.

Fold in half lengthways, wrong side together and press.

Ensure that your project or quilt has been squared up and then attach your binding.

Start at the middle of one edge (I usually start at the bottom). Leave 5" of binding not stitched down. Stitch with the raw edges of the binding to the raw edge of the quilt. Stitch through all the layers. When you approach the corner, stop ¼" from the end. Lift your presser foot and pull quilt out, do not cut the threads. Fold the binding strip laying upward and lining up with the raw edge of the quilt. Hold the fold and lay the binding strip back down in line with the edge of the quilt (see diagrams) continue stitching. You should still be stitching on the raw edge of the binding and the quilt. When you get back to near where you started stop, leaving a 3-5" gap. Measure your binding, connect your ends and trim. Finger press the seam open and continue to stitch in place. Fold your binding over to the back side of your quilt and hand stitch into place, mitre your corners as you go.

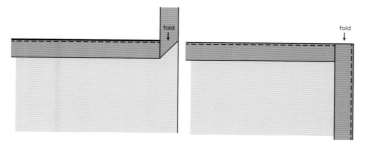

METRIC CONVERSION CHART

TO CONVERT	TO	MULTIPLY BY
inches	cm	2.54
cm	inches	0.4
feet	cm	30.5
cm	feet	0.03
yards	meters	0.9
meters	yards	1.1

GLOSSARY OF TERMS

RST - Right Sides Together
WOF - Width of Fabric
EPP - English Paper Piecing
HST - Half Square Triangle

All seam allowances are ¼" unless stated otherwise

PROJECTS

STRAWBERRY AND CREAM CLAM SHELL DILLY BAG

I love to travel with a little "hand made" and this gorgeous Dilly Bag is perfect for personal effects.

FINISHED MEASUREMENTS
Approximately 6 ¾" x 9 ¾"

SHAPE REQUIRED

▶ 2" clamshells x 50
▶ Trace the "Dilly Bag Base" (found in the template section) onto cardstock.

FABRIC REQUIREMENTS

▶ Fabric scraps for 50 x 2" clamshells

LINEN

▶ 23" x 6" top of clamshells (a)
▶ 23" x 1 ½" bottom of clamshells (b)
▶ Cut 1 "Dilly Bag Base" using the cardstock template (c)

LINING

▶ 10 ¾" x 21" lining (d)
▶ 8" x 21" pocket (e)
▶ Cut 1 "Dilly Bag Base" using the cardstock template (f)
▶ 2" x 10" drawstring casing (g) x 2
▶ 23" cotton lace trim
▶ 70" cording
▶ 10 ¾" x 21" of parlan
▶ Cut 1 "Base Template" (found in the template section) from template plastic (h)
▶ Cut 2 "Dilly Bag Base" using the cardstock template from scrap batting (i)

1 Cut and prepare fifty (50), 2" Clamshells - see "Fussy cutting" and "Glue basting curves" in the techniques section.

2 Refer to "Joining your pieces – clamshells" in the Techniques section and sew 5 strips of 10 clam shells.

For this project the clamshells will interlock at the back of the Dilly bag therefore it is important to leave some clamshell papers in place. Leave the first clamshell paper in the 2nd and 4th rows and leave the last clam shell paper in the 1st, 3rd and 5th row.

Sew your first row of clamshells to the 23" x 6" piece of linen (a), centering your string of 10 clamshells on the linen. Continue to sew all 5 rows.

Once finished, lay your work right sides facing up and it should look like this when you fold the edges in.

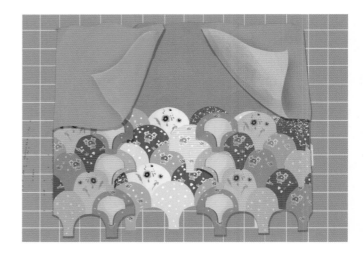

3 With your rotary cutter and ruler trim off the bottom of the last row of clamshells as pictured.

4 With your sewing machine, attach the 23" x 1.5" linen (b) to the bottom of your panel and press with your iron. Pin and attach the 23" piece of cotton lace trim at the bottom of the clamshells, over the seam.

5 Fold the linen under at the outer edge of the two clamshells on the top row. Press and pin as pictured.

6 Sew the clamshell edges together, interlocking them.

Tuck and pin the bottom lace and linen under to form a seam ready to be machine sewn.

7 Turn your unit inside out and remove the remaining papers. Remove the pins and line up the ironed, folded lines at the top and the bottom, re-pin and sew the seam with your sewing machine.

8 With your rotary cutter and ruler, trim away the excess fabric ¼" from the seam. You now have the tube of your Dilly Bag.

9 Now to add the base. Fold your linen base into quarters and press with your iron. Fold and mark the quarter way marks with pins on the bottom of the body of the bag.

10 Line up the quarter marks on the bag and base and pin into place with right sides facing. Take it to your sewing machine and sew.

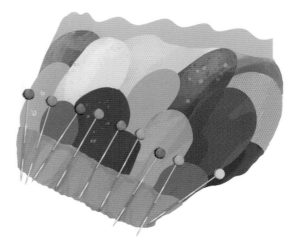

11 To make the Dilly Bag lining:

A- Take the pocket fabric (e) and fold in half lengthways to make a piece 4" x 21" and press. Top stitch ¼" down from the fold.

B- Iron a piece of parlan to the back of the lining fabric (d).

C- Lay the pocket (e) across the bottom of the lining fabric (d) and pin into place.

D- With a water erasable fabric pen, draw lines at 5.5", 10.5" and 15.5" on the pocket fabric, and then with your sewing machine sew along the drawn line to create the internal pockets.

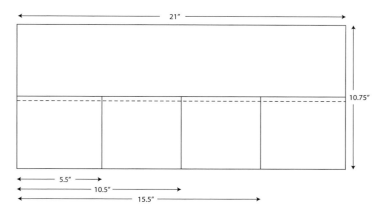

E- Face the two 10 ¾" sides right sides together and sew with your sewing machine, leaving a 5" turning gap in the seam for turning.

F- Repeat steps 9 and 10 to attach your internal base (f).

12 Turn the clamshell component inside out and slide in your lining component facing right sides out (both right sides of fabric should now be facing each other), pin and sew around the top. Turn your bag right sides out through the turning gap.

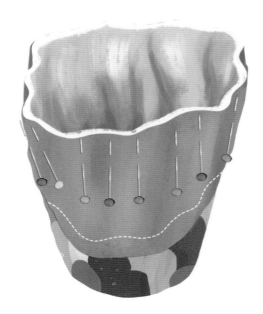

13 With your sewing machine, top stitch ¼" down from the top to create a neat finish.

DRAWSTRING CASINGS

14 Take the two drawstring casings (g) and fold the long edges to the center and press, making a 1" strip. Unfold and then fold the 2" ends over ¼" and press. Fold over ¼" again, press and then topstitch with your sewing machine.

15 Lay the Dilly Bag flat with the center seam to the back. Position a drawstring casing 1 ½" down from the top of the bag and centered widthways. Pin into place. Repeat for the back. Position the bag over the arm of your

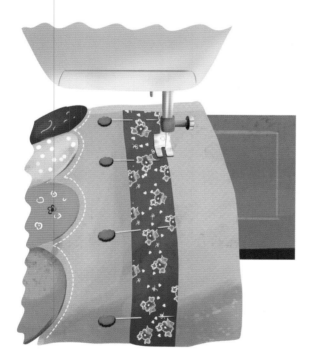

16 Cut your cord in half. Feed one piece through one side of the casing, loop and feed through the back casing, tying the ends in a knot. Repeat for the other half of the cord, this time feeding it through from the opposite side and around. Tie the end.

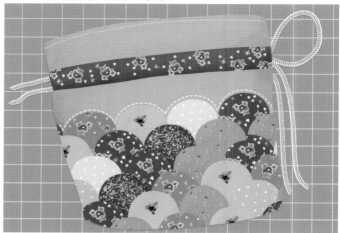

17 Sandwich the template plastic base (h) between the two Dilly Bag bases (i) cut from scrap batting. Carefully pin into place, centering the template plastic. With your sewing machine, carefully stitch around the batting, ensuring that you do not stitch through the template plastic.

Carefully slide the covered template plastic base through the turning gap in the lining and position it on the bottom of the bag. To hold into place, secure it with a few stitches through the lining to the base.

18 Using a whip stitch – see "Hand stitches" in the Techniques section - sew the turning gap in the lining closed.

RADIANT QUILT

I love to see my family wrapped in a handmade quilt and "Radiant" was designed with loved ones in mind. A simple quilt with repeating blocks and simple shapes that can be fussy cut (or not). This quilt can easily be made bigger or smaller depending on who you are making it for. Wrap a loved one in quilty love.

FINISHED MEASUREMENTS
53 ¼" x 53 ¼"

SHAPES REQUIRED

- 2" square x 128
- 4-point star x 128
- Radiant kite x 128
- Setting square x 25
- Filler polygon blocks x 80

FABRIC REQUIREMENTS

- FQ small blue floral
- 1 ¼" yard small red floral
- ½ yard large blue floral
- ½ yard large pink floral
- 10" x WOF green
- 25" x WOF red stripe
- 30" x WOF white spot background

CUTTING INSTRUCTIONS

- 1st border (red stripe) cut 5 x 1 ½" WOF
- 2nd border (red floral) cut 5 x 5 ½" WOF
- Binding (red stripe)
- Cut 6 x 2 ½" WOF
- Background fabric (white with white spot)
- Cut 8 x 3 ¼" WOF

I have fussy cut this quilt but it does not have to be. If you are, please see "Fussy cutting" in the Techniques section.

1 For each block cut and prepare,
- 4-point star pieces x 8 (4 in red and 4 in blue)
- Radiant kite pieces x 8 (in green)
- 2" squares x 8 (4 in blue and 4 in pink)

See "Glue basting" in the Techniques section. For the finished quilt as pictured you need 16 blocks.

2 Assemble your center 4-point stars – see "Joining" in the Techniques section.

3 Lay out the remaining pieces for your block and English Paper Piece them together.

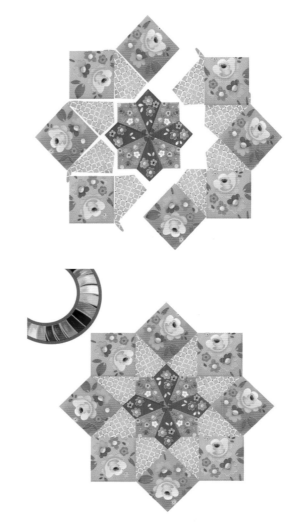

Make 16 blocks.

4 Preparing your borders. Take your previously cut 3 ¼" WOF strips of white background fabric.

If you have a nice sharp blade in your rotary cutter you will be able to layer a few strips on top of each other.

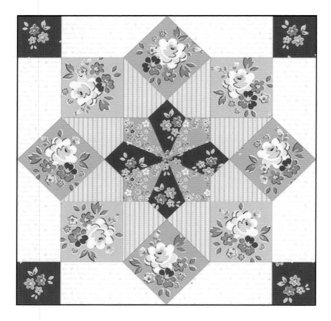

Lay one of your filler polygon paper pieces, centered as pictured and using your add-a-quarter ruler cut your pieces ¼" larger than the papers.

NOTE: There are two filler polygon blocks. One is used in between the blocks in the main body of your quilt. It has one flat edge and one pointy edge. The other has a triangle missing on the corner. These are used for the outer border pieces only.

5 Flip your paper to the other side and repeat. Continue and cut 48.

6 Repeat steps 4 and 5 for the outer filler polygon block – with the corner still attached.

These are used for the outer most edge of your quilt before the borders are added. Cut 32.

7 Prepare 25 Setting Squares. These can be strip cut from 3 ½" strips. See "strip cutting" in the Techniques section.

8 Start adding your filler polygon pieces to your blocks and build your quilt, remembering to remove your papers as you go.

9 When you have the inside section/the English Paper Pieced section of your quilt all pieced, remove all the remaining papers, fold out the seam allowance and press.

10 To add your first border (red stripe), take your 1 ½" x WOF strips and piece 2 strips to the length of 42". Pin, and use your sewing machine to sew to the sides of your quilt. Press.

11 Piece together your 1 ½" strips to make two border strips 44 ½" in length. Pin, and use your sewing machine to sew to the top and bottom of your quilt. Press.

12 Repeat steps 10 and 11 with your second 5 ½" border fabric but this time, make two strips at 44 ½" for the sides and two at 55" in length for the top and bottom.

13 Quilt as desired – see "Quilting" in the techniques section. I had mine professionally quilted.

FLOWER GARDEN MINI QUILT

Hexagons were the first shape that I ever played with when learning to English Paper Piece. I love the traditional feel that they have.

FINISHED MEASUREMENTS
Approximately 21 ½" x 23 ½"

SHAPE REQUIRED

▶ ¾" hexagons (271)

FABRIC REQUIREMENTS

▶ Various FQ's for your flowers
▶ 1 FQ of background fabrics
▶ 27" square piece of backing fabric
▶ 27" square of parlan or batting
▶ 85" picot edge binding

1 Fussy cut and prepare:

- ¾" hexagons x 49 (7 for each of the 7 flowers)
- ¾" hexagons x 12 (to surround the flowers)
- ¾" hexagons x 114 (for the background)
- ¾" hexagons x 24 (4 for each corner unit - 1 fussy cut and 3 stripe)

See "Fussy cutting" and "Glue basting" in the Techniques section.

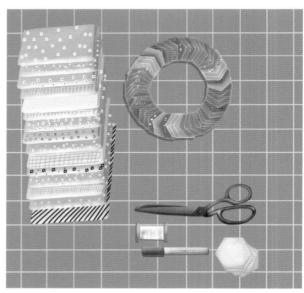

2 English Paper Piece your hexagons into flowers and then add a second round - see "Sewing your pieces" in the Techniques section.

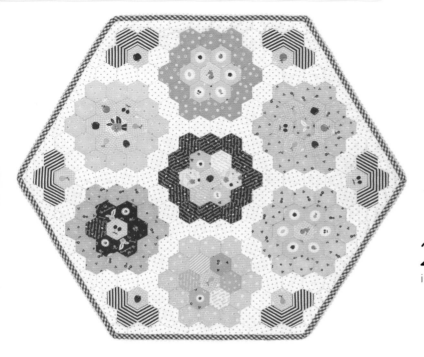

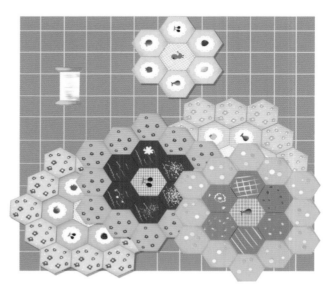

3 Lay for flowers out in a pleasing manner and begin to surround them with the background hexagons, joining in the flowers as you go.

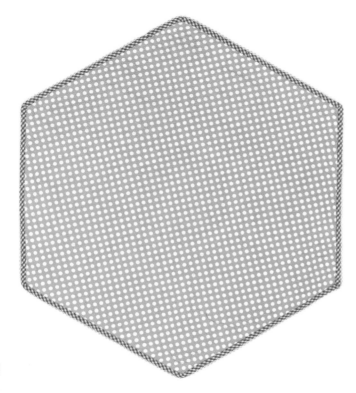

4   Piece the six corner units and sew them to the larger flower unit as pictured.

5   Remove all of the papers and press with your iron.

6   Create a quilt sandwich and quilt as desired – see "Quilting" in the Techniques section.

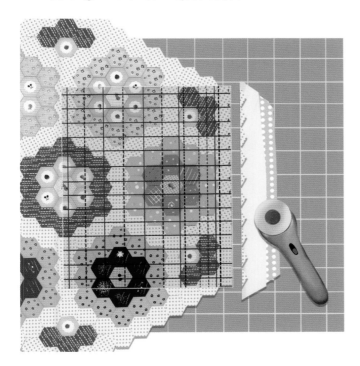

7   Trim ¾" out from the points of your Hexagons with your rotary cutter and ruler.

8   Bind with angled mitred corners.

Take the width of your folded binding, for example 1 ¼", and draw the two intersecting lines, 1 ¼" away from the edge as pictured.

Sew the binding as per the "Binding" instructions in the Techniques section. Using a ¼" seam, sew to the point at the corner where the two lines intersect. Fold your binding back along the stitching line to align the raw edge with the next side of the quilt. Fold the binding down so that the fold aligns with the outer point of the quilt. Beginning at the top edge of the quilt begin sewing again, catching the fold of the binding in your stitching.

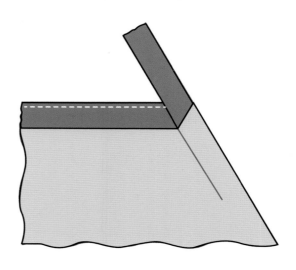

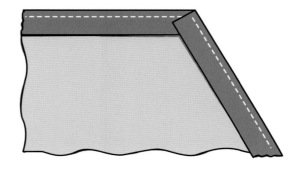

SUMMER STAR TABLE RUNNER

It is the little touches within a house that makes it a home.

FINISHED MEASUREMENTS
Approximately 31 ½" x 12 ¼"

SHAPES REQUIRED

▸ 2" 8-pointed star x 48
▸ 2" square x 44

FABRIC REQUIREMENTS

▸ Various fabrics for fussy cutting, diamonds and squares
▸ 14" x WOF Background Fabric (Aqua Spot)
▸ From your background fabric cut 1 ½" x WOF (x 3) and set aside for your border
▸ 90" binding
▸ 34" x 15" piece of batting/parlan
▸ 34" x 15" piece of backing fabric

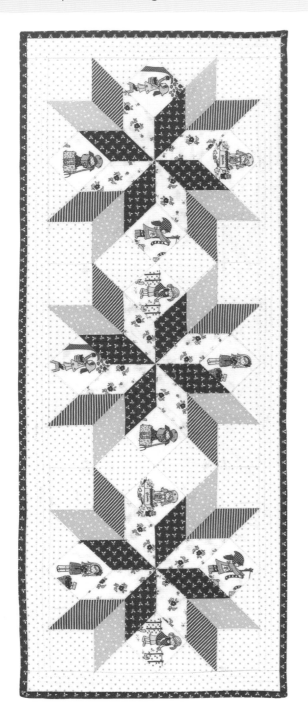

This Table Runner can be broken down into three sections.

1 For each section cut and prepare your pieces. Refer to "Fussy Cutting" and "Basting" in the Techniques Section.

In total you need to prepare: -

- 2" 8-point stars x 12 (dark red)
- 2" 8-point stars x 12 (white floral)
- 2" 8-point stars x 12 (red stripe)
- 2" 8-point stars x 12 (aqua)
- 2" fussy cut squares x 12
- 2" squares in background fabric x 12 (aqua spot)

See "Fussy cutting" and "Glue basting" in the Techniques section.

2 Begin to piece the individual sections of your table runner – see 'Joining the pieces' in the Techniques section, taking note of how to join diamonds/stars. Once you have made the three sections, proceed to join them together.

3 Remove all remaining papers and press with your iron, folding out your seam allowance. Refer 'Including EPP in any project' in the Techniques section.

4 With your rotary cutter and ruler, trim away the excess triangles from your edge squares, ensuring that you leave ¼" from the points of the star pieces.

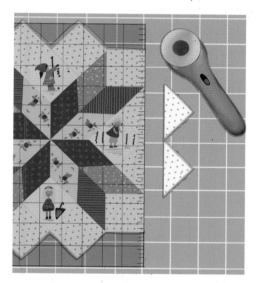

5 Measure the length of your table runner and cut two strips of this length from your pre-cut 1 ½" background fabric. Pin one strip to the top and one to the bottom of your table runner and attach with your sewing machine. Press.

6 Measure the width of your table runner and again cut two strips to this length from your pre-cut 1 ½" background fabric. Pin, and use your sewing machine to sew one strip to each side. Press.

7 Make a quilt sandwich and quilt as desired – see "Quilting" in the Techniques section.

8 Trim away the excess batting and backing fabric. Prepare and attach your binding - see "Binding" in the Techniques section.

CELESTIAL STAR

From a very young age I was drawn to the brightest star in the sky at night. I would lay in the middle of our back yard looking up, taking in all the beauty and wonderment of above. "Celestial Star" has been inspired by these mid-summers nights.

FINISHED MEASUREMENTS
59 ¼" Square

SHAPES REQUIRED

- ▶ Celestial octagon
- ▶ Celestial star wing
- ▶ Celestial star jewel
- ▶ Celestial kite
- ▶ 4-point star
- ▶ Isosceles triangle
- ▶ Diamond filler
- ▶ Triangle filler

Celestial Star is a great chance to play with your fussy cutting, although this quilt does not have to be. If you do choose to fussy cut, this quilt truly does allow you the opportunity to create a quilt that is unique to you by the way you fussy cut your chosen fabrics.

I have used predominately Liberty fabrics in my quilt. What may not be obvious from looking at this quilt is that the octagons and celestial star jewel shapes within the orange, red, purple, green and blue star bursts have ALL been cut from the same fabric.

Celestial Star is made from two units. The 'Color Bursts' and the 'Star Bursts'.

CELESTIAL STAR

FABRIC REQUIREMENTS

Due to the nature of this project and the fussy cutting, exact fabric requirements can not be given. I have provided a guide based on what I used and this will vary depending on the spacing in the repeats of your chosen fabrics.

When selecting your fabrics, please remember that this pattern works on a repeat of 8.

TIP: If you know that you are going to be fussy cutting a fabric at the time of purchase I would recommend always getting a little bit more than you think you will use just to be sure. I have learned the hard way about not buying enough fabric.

FABRIC QUANTITY GUIDE

- ▶ Background - 2 ½" yards white on white spot (includes binding)

COLOR BURSTS

- ▶ 2 yards of the feature fabric for use in the orange, red, blue, green and purple Color Burst
- ▶ 1 FQ each in orange, red, blue, green and purple solid
- ▶ 12" x WOF each in orange, red, blue, green and purple stripe or crosshatch
- ▶ FQ each in orange, red, blue, green and purple for the 4-point stars in the Color Bursts

STAR BURSTS

- ▶ 1 ½" yards yellow for Star Bursts
- ▶ 27" x WOF of 4 different Liberty prints (This made 6 Star Bursts each.)
- ▶ 18" x WOF of 1 Liberty fabric (This made 2 Star bursts)

COLOR BURSTS

- ▶ Make 9 full Color Bursts and 4 corner units.

STAR BURSTS

- ▶ Make 24 Star Burst Units.

INSTRUCTIONS

COLOR BURST UNITS

FOR EACH FULL COLOR BURST CUT AND PREPARE

- Celestial octagon x 1
- Celestial star wing x 16
- Celestial star jewel x 8
- Celestial kite x 8
- 4-point star x 32

Make 9.

**Please pay special attention to your star wings. They are reversible for a left-and right-hand sided wing. There is also a wrong and right way for them to be sewn together.

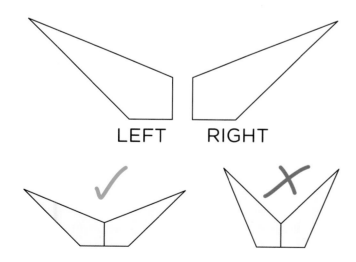

LEFT   RIGHT

FOR EACH CORNER UNIT CUT AND PREPARE

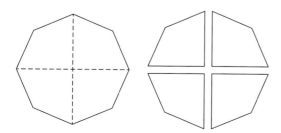

- Celestial octagon (one quarter, cut as pictured)
- Celestial star wing x 4
- Celestial star jewel x 2
- Celestial kite x 3
- 4-point star x 8

Make 4.

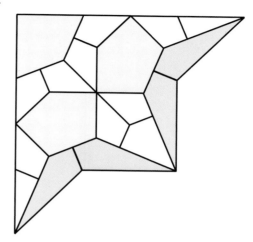

Before you begin to cut and prepare your pieces, you need to decide if you have/are using a directional print for the octagon and pay special attention to the preparation and placement so that your print sits in the right direction.
Attach your 4-point stars to the outside of the octagon. I made units of two and then attached those to the octagon. Add your jewels.

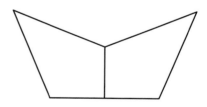

Piece your 4-point stars, kite units and your wing units and add them to your center unit.

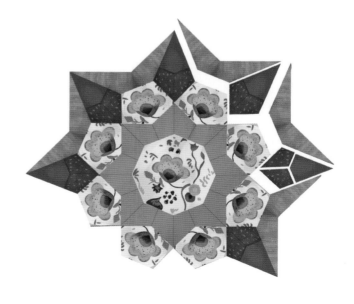

Make 9 complete units and 4 corner units.

STAR BURST UNITS

For each Star Burst cut and prepare:

- Celestial kite x 8
- 4-point star x 16
- Isosceles triangle x 16

Make 24.

See "Fussy cutting" and "Joining your pieces" section in the Techniques section.

I have alternated the yellow points on my Star Bursts as they work their way around the quilt.

Piece your star units, remembering to pay attention to the "Joining your pieces" instructions in the Techniques section.

Continue to build on your work by adding the remaining Color Bursts and Star Units. Pay special attention to placement if you have made your Color Bursts directional. At this point you will also need to prepare eight Diamond Filler pieces.

BUILDING YOUR QUILT

Once you have made a few units you can start to join your units and build your project.

Between each of the Color Bursts you need to add in a Diamond Filler piece. Your partial Color Burst units go in the corner to square up your project.

TIP: Remember to remove the inner paper pieces to make your project easier to handle. You only need to keep the papers in the outer most edge of your work.

Continue to add your Star Bursts around your center Color Burst.

FINISHING THE EDGES

Prepare 16 triangle fillers and more 8 diamond fillers.

Add the triangle and diamond Filler to the edge of the project to level up the edges.

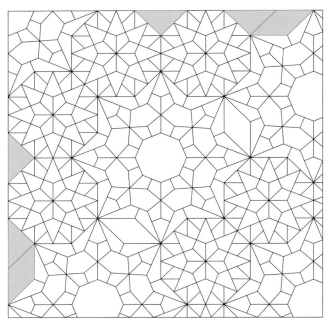

Give your project a light iron and then remove all of the remaining papers - see "Including EPP in any project" in the Techniques section.

Press your project again, folding out the seam allowances. When pressing your edges, leave the fold crease still visible as this helps align you border later, especially of you don't quite have a ¼" seam allowance. Proceed to trim your project.

With your rotary cutter and ruler, trim the edges of your project. You need to be trimming ¼" out from the Star Burst points. This will leave you your quarter inch seam allowance for adding your border.

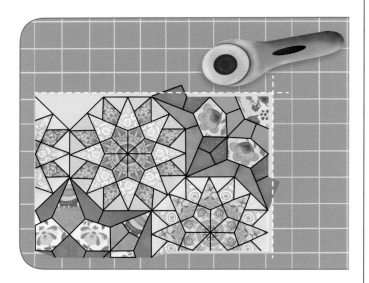

ADDING YOUR BORDER

Your finished English Paper Pieced panel should measure 52" square.

Note: Please check the measurement of your project before proceeding to cut your border fabric. Sometimes a panel can finish a little bigger because it has been stretched during the ironing process. If yours has finished larger please amend the length of your border strips accordingly.

Cut 6 x 5" WOF.

With your sewing machine, piece two lengths at 52" and sew to the top and bottom of your project. Piece two lengths at 61" and sew one to each side of your project.

BINDING

Cut 7 x 2 ½" WOF for the binding.

Quilt and bind as per your preferred method - see "Quilting" and "Binding" in the Techniques section. I had mine professionally quilted in a custom design.

QUILT LAYOUT

TIP: Photocopy this page, grab some pencils and have a play with color and plan your project.

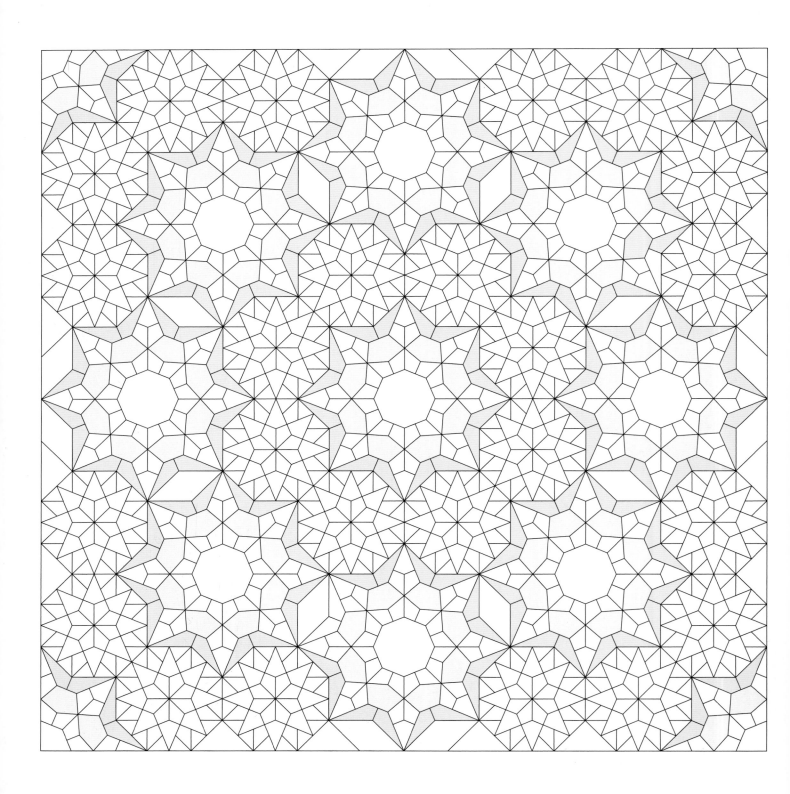

BE MY BUNNY BABY QUILT

Capturing the sweetness of a print and showcasing it is always fun and this cute baby Quilt allows for a cute feature fabric to play centre stage.

FINISHED MEASUREMENTS
Finished size approximately 39 ½" x 39 ½"

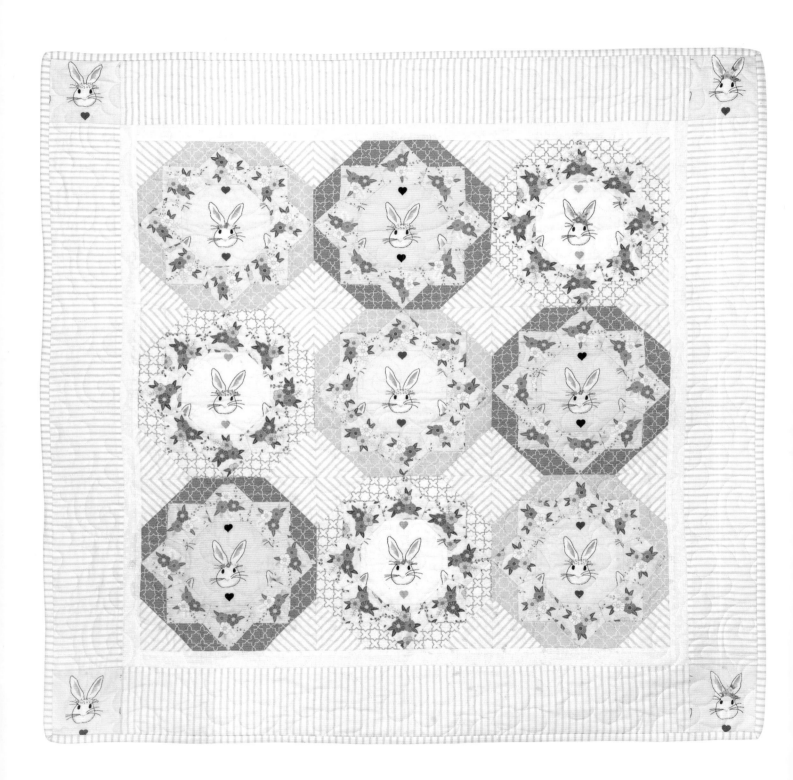

5 Have a play with your layout, and once you are happy with it begin to attach your octagon blocks with your half square triangle units.

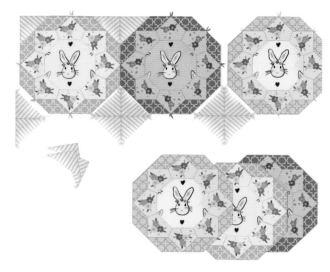

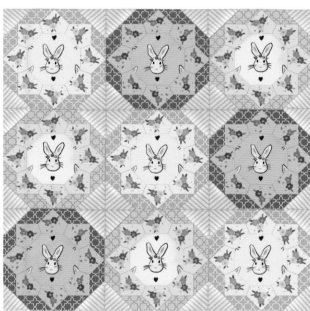

6 Remove all your papers, carefully fold out your seam allowance and press with your iron - see "Including EPP in any project" in the Techniques section.

7 Pin a 1.5" x 29.5" inner border fabric strip to both the top and bottom of your baby quilt and sew with your sewing machine. Pin a 1.5" x 31.5" inner border fabric strip to each side and sew with your sewing machine.

8 Pin and then sew a 4.5" x 31.5" border fabric piece to each side of your baby quilt.

9 Sew a 4 ½" fussy cut corner block to each end of your two remaining 4 ½" x 31 ½" border fabric strips. Pin and then sew one strip to the top and one to the bottom of your baby quilt with your sewing machine.

10 Quilt as desired. I had mine professionally quilted - see "Quilting" in the Techniques section.

11 Prepare and attach your binding – see "Binding" in the Techniques section.

MINI QUILT

Simple in design but play with your fussy cutting mirror and fabric placement on this one and you will be able to achieve so many different results.

FINISHED MEASUREMENTS
Approximately 14 ¼" x 14 ¼"

SHAPES REQUIRED

▸ 2" 8-point Star x 32
▸ 2" square x 16
▸ 2" x 4" rectangle x 4

FABRIC REQUIREMENTS

▸ Various fabrics for fussy cutting.
▸ FQ of background fabric (silver swiss dot)
▸ 65" of 2" binding – see "Binding" in the Techniques section
▸ 16" x 16" batting/parlan
▸ 16" x 16" backing fabric

1 Using your fussy cutting mirror and your perspex templates have a play and explore all of your fussy cutting options from your chosen fabrics – see "Fussy cutting" in the techniques Section.

2 Cut and prepare:

2" 8-point stars in blue x 8
2" 8-point stars in grey x 8
2" 8-point stars in pink x 16
2" squares x 4
2" squares of background fabric x 16
2" x 4" rectangles x 4

See "Glue Basting" in the Techniques section.

3 Begin to piece together your Mini Quilt – see "Joining your Pieces" in the Techniques section and the note on joining stars/diamonds.

There is no right or wrong way to piece your mini as long as you ensure that you piece your center star in two halves and then join. I like to piece in sections and then piece those sections together.

4 Give your work a press with your iron.

5 Remove your papers and unfold your seam allowance. Give your panel a light press. – see "Including EPP in any project" in the Techniques section.

6 Make a quilt sandwich and quilt as desired – see "Quilting" in the Techniques section.

7 With your rotary cutter and ruler, trim your mini quilt. You want to trim ¼" away from the points on your outer stars.

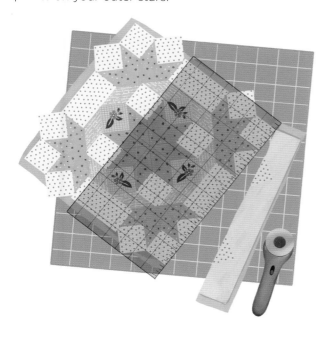

8 Prepare and attach your binding – see "Binding" in the Techniques section.

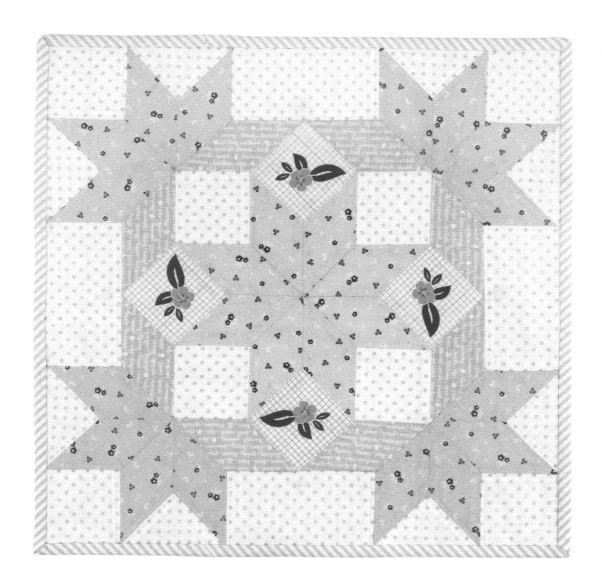

STAR CUSHION

Proving that not everything needs to
be fussy cut is this simple Star Cushion
in pretty florals.

FINISHED MEASUREMENTS
Cushion Finishes at 19 ¾" Square

SHAPES REQUIRED

▸ 2" 6-point star x 48

FABRIC REQUIREMENTS

6 F8's will be more than enough for your stars and squares if you are not fussy cutting.

▸ 2 ½" squares x 36
▸ 1 FQ background Fabric
  subcut 2 ½" x 12 ½" strips x 2
  subcut 2 ½" x 16 ½" strips x 2
  subcut 2" 6-point stars x 17
▸ 20 ½" x 15" rectangles (cushion back) x 2
▸ 22" x 22" piece parlan
▸ DMC Perle thread 12 in white
▸ Size 20 cushion insert

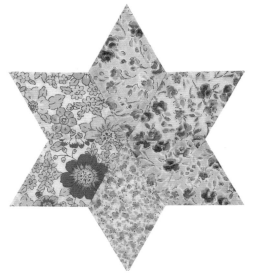

1 Prepare 31 printed diamonds for the featured stars and 17 diamonds of your background fabrics – see "Glue basting" in the Techniques section.

2 Sew together three full stars and two partial stars with only 4 points – see "Joining your pieces" in the Techniques section.

3 Piece a panel as pictured by surrounding your stars with the background diamonds. Press.

4 Remove papers and unfold your seam allowance. Press with your iron. With your quilting ruler and rotary cutter, trim edges ¼" out from the points. Your panel should measure 12 ½" square

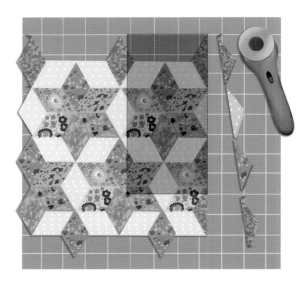

5 With your sewing machine, pin and sew one of the 2 ½" x 12 ½" rectangles to the top and one to the bottom of your star panel. Press with your iron. Pin and sew one of the ½" x 16 ½" rectangles to each side of your star panel. Press with your iron.

6 Lay your 2 ½" squares around your cushion panel and play with the layout. When you are happy, sew the eight squares for the top row together and eight for the bottom. Sew the top and bottom rows to your star panel and press. Repeat the process for the ten squares each side and attach.

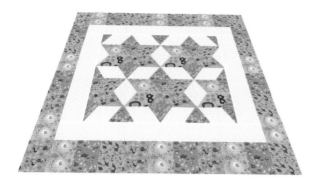

7 Iron on a piece of parlan to the wrong side of your panel and quilt as desired. I have hand quilted mine. See "Quilting" in the Techniques section.

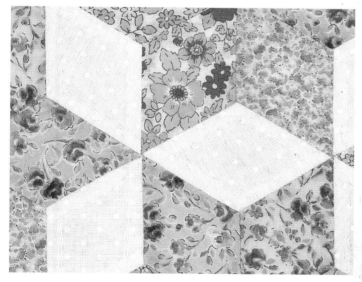

8 Trim away the excess parlan with your ruler and rotary cutter.

CUSHION BACK

9 On each of the two 20 ½" x 15" rectangles fold the long edge over ½" and press. Fold over again another ½" and press. Take to your sewing machine and top stitch.

ASSEMBLE YOUR CUSHION

10 Lay your cushion front right side up. Place one of the backing pieces to the left-hand side, lining up the raw edges. Repeat for the right-hand side, overlapping the two backing pieces in the middle.

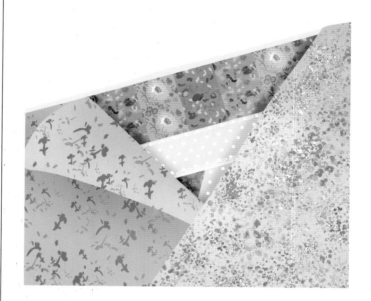

11 Pin the layers together. Take to your sewing machine and sew around all the edges with a ¼" seam allowance, removing the pins as you go. Sew around again, this time with a zigzag/overlocking stitch.

12 Turn right sides out. Press and insert your cushion insert.

SWEET WOODLAND BUNTING

A perfect project for small-scale prints and what little girl wouldn't love a flower bunting in her own room.

FINISHED MEASUREMENTS
Finished length approximately 85 ¾"

SHAPES REQUIRED

▸ 5/8" hexagon x 9
▸ 5/8" hexagon flower petal x 54
▸ Trace the "Bunting" template (found in the template section) onto cardstock.

FABRIC REQUIREMENTS

▸ Various fabrics for fussy cutting your flowers
▸ 20" pink gingham
▸ 13" solid pink for the back of your bunting
▸ 64" cotton lace or trim
▸ 6 ½" x 8" parlan (thin fusible batting) x 9
▸ DMC embroidery floss B5200 in white

CUTTING INSTRUCTIONS

▸ Pink gingham – cut 2 6 ½" x WOF
sub cut into 9 6 ½" x 8" rectangles
Cut 2 3 ½" x WOF

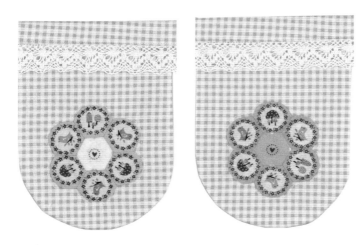

1 Cut and prepare 9 complete hexagon flowers – See "Fussy cutting", "Glue basting" and "Joining your pieces" in the Techniques section. Press your English Paper Pieced flowers with a warm iron. Remove the papers and, if needed, repress with your iron.

FOR EACH FLOWER

Apply a little appliqué glue to the back of your hexagon flower where indicated (you only need a very small amount).

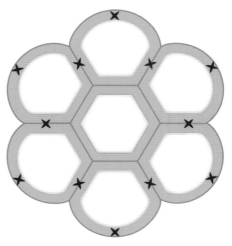

2 Position the flower onto a pink gingham rectangle with the center hexagon approximately 3" up from the bottom.

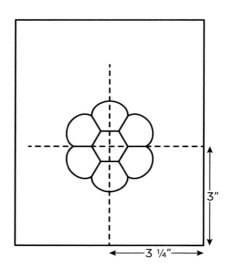

3 Allow the glue to dry or alternatively press gently with a warm iron to speed up the drying process. Appliqué your flower onto the background using a blind stitch - see "Hand stitches"in the Technique section. Once completed, iron a piece of parlan to the back of your work.

4 Centering the cardstock bunting template over your pink gingham/flowers, use a pencil or erasable fabric pen and trace. Cut out along the outer template line.

5 Add a running stitch around your flowers – see "Hand stitches" in the Techniques section.

6 Cut 9 bunting templates from your solid pink fabric.

7 Place your gingham flowers and pink solid fabric right sides together and pin. With your sewing machine, sew ¼" around the outside, leaving the top open.

8 Carefully, with your scissors, clip your seam alowance at ¼" intervals around the curve. Do not cut through the sewn line. Turn right side out and press.

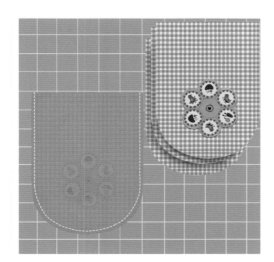

9 Measuring from the curved bottom up, trim to a height of 7".

10 Join your two 3 ½" WOF strips together, forming one long strip.

11 Fold in half lengthways and press with your iron. Fold both edges into the center and press again. Fold the short ends in ½" and iron.

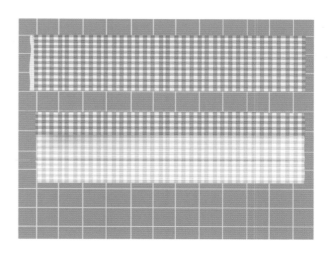

12 Find the center of your cotton Lace and the casing. Position a bunting flower in the casing and pin into place. Working each way, leave a gap of 2" and position the next bunting flower, layering the lace and pinning as you go.

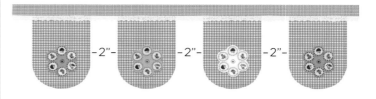

13 With your sewing machine, sew your bunting flowers and lace within the casing. At the first and last bunting flower, fold the lace trim to the back, fold over and hand stitch into place for a neat finished look.

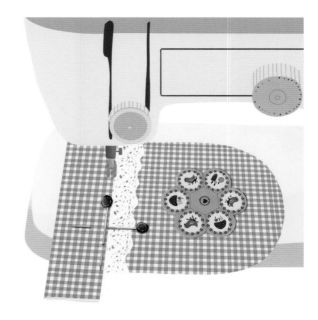

PATCHWORK BLOCK KEEPER

I am always in my sewing studio making a creative mess with many projects on the go at one time. This fun patchwork block keeper allows me to keep all my completed quilt blocks together, protected and looking pretty at the same time.

FINISHED MEASUREMENTS
Approximately 13 ¾" x 13 ¾"

SHAPES REQUIRED

▸ 2" 8-pointed star x 32
▸ 2" square x 28

FABRIC REQUIREMENTS

▸ Various fabrics for fussy cutting
▸ 3" x 14 ½" (internal and external spine) x 2
▸ 14.5" x 14 ½" (inside and back) x 3
▸ 12" x 14 ½" (inside pockets) x 2
▸ 2" x WOF (ties)
▸ 100" binding
▸ 33" x 16 ½" soft 'n' stable x 1
▸ 26" x 13" batting (book pages) x 5
▸ 12 ½" x 13" template plastic – optional x 2

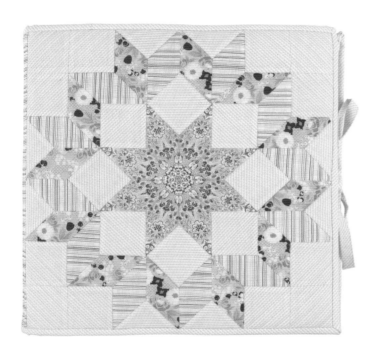

1 Using your fussy cutting mirror and your perspex templates have a play and explore all your fussy cutting options from your chosen fabrics. The center of this project is a great chance to play with the kaleidoscope effects by cutting on repeat – see "Fussy cutting" in the Techniques section.

2 Cut and prepare:

2" 8-point stars x 32
2" squares x 28
See "Glue basting" in the Techniques section.

3 Begin to piece your panel, remembering to piece the center star pieces in 2 halves before joining - see "Joining your pieces" in the Techniques section.

4 With your iron, press your block and remove your papers, folding the seam allowance out. Trim the overhang with your rotary cutter and ruler ensuring you leave ¼" from the points for your seam allowance.

5 Take one 14 ½" x 14 ½" (back) and sew a 3" x 14 ½" (spine) to the right-hand side and then sew your English Paper Pieced block to the right. The unit should measure 31" x 14 ½". Baste this section with the soft 'n' stable and quilt as desired. I have done some simple straight line quilting with the walking foot on my sewing machine, – see "Quilting" in the Techniques section.

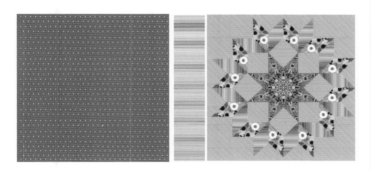

6 Trim the excess soft 'n' stable away using your rotary cutter and ruler.

7 Take your 12" x 14 ½" pocket fabric and fold in half, wrong sides together, and iron the fold. Top stitch ¼" from the fold with your sewing machine.

8 Layer your two pockets over the 14 ½" x 14 ½" inside panels and pin into place.

9 Pin the spine to one side and sew with your sewing machine. Repeat for the right-hand side making one panel that measures 31" x 14 ½".

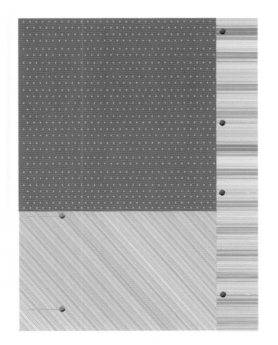

10 Pin the inside panel to the wrong side of the quilted front panel, lining up the spines. Your inside panel will be a little larger than your quilted panel (the quilting shrinks it ever so slightly), We will trim this in step 13.

11 With your sewing machine, top stitch around the outer edge of the panels approximately ⅛" from the edge leaving the back right hand edge open.

(Optional) Slide in a piece of template plastic through the opening left unstitched and slide it over to be in the front cover part of your block keeper and with your sewing machine stitch down both sides of the spine. (The template plastic is smaller than the cover size.) DO NOT try to stitch through the template plastic.

12 Slide the other piece of template plastic into the back cover and with your sewing machine stitch closed with a ⅛" seam.

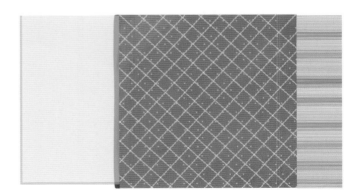

13 Trim away the excess from the outer edges.

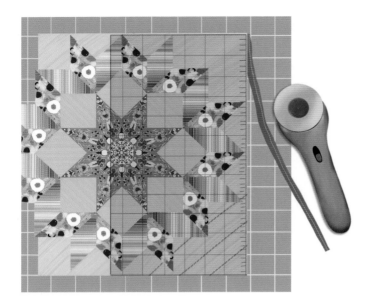

15 Make the ties by folding the 2" x WOF strip in half wrong sides together and press with your iron. Open and fold in each edge to the middle and press with your iron. Top stitch the opening closed with your sewing machine. Cut the length in half and tie a knot in one end of each tie.

16 Attach one to the inside front cover, half way down and repeat for the other on the inside of the back cover.

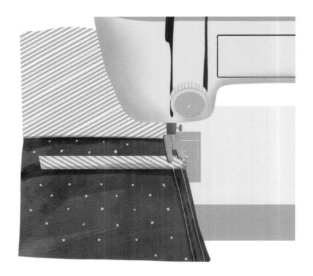

14 Fold two of the batting pages in half and pin approximately ½" in from the left of the spine and with your sewing machine, sew down the middle of the pages to secure them in place. Repeat and sew two pages to the right-hand side of the spine, again ½" in, and then sew the last page into the middle.

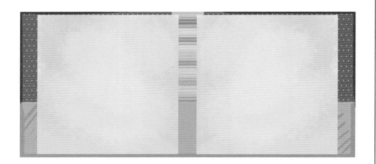

17 Make and attach your binding – see "Binding" in the Techniques section.

ZIPPER POUCH

This project is inspired by beautiful sunrises over Australian beaches, especially in summer.

FINISHED MEASUREMENTS
Approximately 10 ¼" x 6 ¼"

SHAPES USED

- ▸ 2" rounded dresden x 6
- ▸ 2" pointed dresden x 6
- ▸ 1½" circle x 1

FABRIC REQUIREMENTS

- ▸ Various fabrics for fussy cutting the dresden plates
- ▸ 11" x 4½" white on white spot (a) x 2
- ▸ 11" x 4" rose gold (b) x 2
- ▸ 11" x 8" lining fabric (c) x 2
- ▸ 2" squares for zip ends (d) x2
- ▸ white 14" zip x 1
- ▸ 11" x 8" parlan (thin fusible web) x 2
- ▸ DMC embroidery thread (color 951)
- ▸ Optional zip charm

1 Fussy cut and prepare:
- Rounded Dresden x 6
- Pointed Dresden x 6
- 1 ½" Circle x 1

See "Fussy cutting" and "Glue basting" and "Glue basting curves" in the Techniques section. Note: You don't need to baste the bottom of the dresdens as these will be covered by the circle.

2 Refer to the "Joining your pieces" in the Techniques section and sew your rounded and pointed dresden's into two semicircles. Press your dresdens and circle with a warm iron. Remove the papers from your Dresdens.

3 Take your rounded dresden semicircle and apply a few tiny dots of appliqué glue to the seam allowance on the back side. Turn the dresdens over and position the dresden plate approximately 1" in from the left side of one of the white (a) fabric panels and aligned with the bottom of fabric (a).

4 Allow the glue to dry or alternatively press gently with a warm iron to speed up the drying process.

5 Repeat steps 4 and 5 for the pointed dresden, this time centering it on top of the rounded dresden.

6 Appliqué the dresden plates to the background and each other using a blind stitch – see "Hand stitches" in the Techniques section. Then appliqué the circle over the center, remove the paper and trim off the overhang.

7 With your sewing machine, sew your 11" x 4 ½" (a) fabric to your 11" x 4" (b) fabric along the long edge forming a panel measuring 11" x 8".

8 Iron on a piece of parlan to the back of each panel.

9 Cut a 1 ½" square from the bottom left and right from each of your outside pouch panels and the lining.

10 With your sewing machine, top stitch along the seam on the front and back panels for your pouch. Add a running stitch detail around the outer edge of your dresdens using a double strand of coordinating DMC thread – see "Hand stitches" in the Techniques section.

11 On the front and back external panels, with a water erasable fabric marker, mark the ¼" seam allowance at the top on both sides.

12 Remove the metal tab at the end of your zip and then, with your sewing machine, zigzag the end closed. (This is an optional step but it is something that I like to do with my zips. It helps remove a little bulk and eliminates the chance of accidently hitting the needle on my machine against the metal tab, causing damage.)

13 Take your two 2" (d) squares and iron them in half, then iron one end into the middle.

14 Lay one square right side up and place the zip on top as pictured, and with your sewing machine stitch into place.

15 Fold over, pin and top stitch.

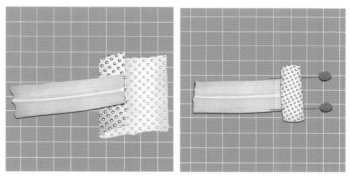

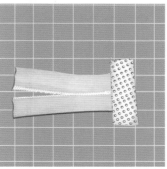

16 Position your zip above the top of your front panel and trim it so it is just shorter than the ¼" mark made in step 11. Then repeat steps 14 and 15. Trim the excess off once finished.

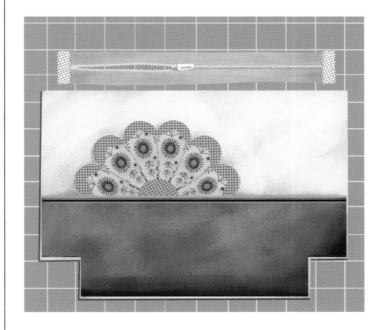

ATTACHING THE ZIP

17 Position your pouch front right side up and place the zip on the top, right side down, positioning it in between the marks made in step 11. Lay the lining right side down. Line up all the tops, pin and sew into place using the zipper foot on your sewing machine.

When completed you can see that your zip will fit inside the ¼" seam allowance.

18 Lay the back of your zipper pouch right side up and position the zip facing down, again positioning between the marks made in Step 11 and then position the lining on top, also facing right sides down. Align all the top edges, pin and sew. Whilst you still have your zipper foot on your sewing machine, top stitch along each side of the zip, ensuring that the lining is out of the way.

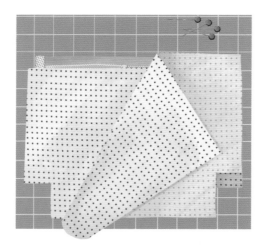

19 Open the zip all the way. Lay your pouch with the right sides of the exterior facing each other and the lining facing each other, pin. With your sewing machine, sew along all the edges leaving a 4" gap in the lining seam to allow you to turn your pouch inside out when finished.

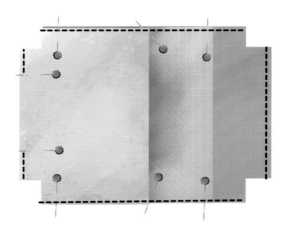

20 Hold and pin the pouch ends so that the side seams align and the corner cut out makes a straight line. Sew with your sewing machine. Repeat for all 4 corners.

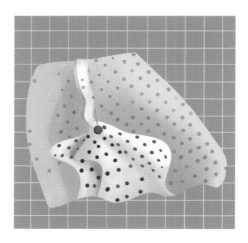

21 Turn your pouch the right way out through the gap left in the lining seam. Using a whip stitch sew the turning gap closed. See "Hand stitches" in the Techniques section.

You will see that the tabs at each end of your zip sit nice and flat just inside the side seams.

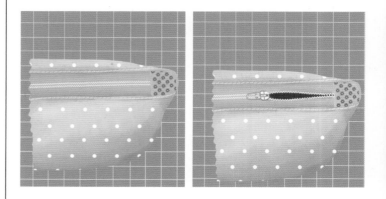

SEW SWEET PINCUSHION AND NEEDLE KEEPER

A sweet gift for a sewing friend or just for you. Either way I feel that one can never have enough home-made Pincushions and Needle Keepers.

FINISHED MEASUREMENTS
Needle Keeper
Approximately 4 ″ x 4 ¼″
Pincushion
Approximately 3 ¼″ x 1 ½″

SHAPES REQUIRED

▸ 1" scallop x 9
▸ ⅝" hexagon x 7
▸ Trace the "Pincushion Top" template (found in the template section) onto cardstock.

FABRIC REQUIREMENTS

▸ Various fabrics for fussy cutting the scallops and hexagons

NEEDLE KEEPER

▸ 5" square of background fabric
▸ 1 ½" X 4 ½" rectangle of stripe fabric
▸ 4 ½" Square for the back
▸ 4 ½" x 9 ½" fusible interfacing
▸ 4 ½" x 9 ½" pocket fabric
▸ 4 ½" x 9 ½" inside lining fabric
▸ 3 ½" x 7 ½" white felt x 2
▸ 9" length ⅜" wide ribbon
▸ 1 small pair of embroidery scissors
▸ 2 small buttons
▸ Buttons and trims to embellish
▸ Coordinating DMC thread

PIN CUSHION

▸ 3" x 11" rectangle low volume fabric
▸ 3" x 11" fusible interfacing
▸ Cut 1 pincushion top using the cardstock template
▸ 2 ½" x 4" rectangles for pincushion base x 2
▸ Preferred pincushion stuffing (wadding/toy stuffing or crushed walnut shells)

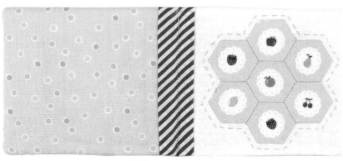

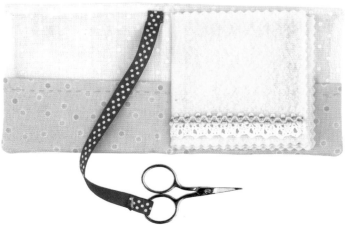

INSTRUCTIONS

NEEDLE KEEPER

1 Fussy cut and prepare: ⅝" hexagons x 7
See "Fussy cutting" and "Glue basting" in the Techniques section.

2 English Paper Piece your hexagons into a flower. Press and then remove the papers. - see "Joining your pieces" in the Techniques section.

3 Fold your background fabric into quarters and press. Using these guide lines, appliqué your flower onto your background fabric by placing small dots of appliqué glue on the wrong side of your flower and then positioning onto your background fabric. Allow to air dry, or alternatively gently press with your iron to speed up the drying process. Using a blind stitch (see "Hand stitches" in Techniques section) appliqué into place.

4 Trim your square back to 4 ½", ensuring your flower is in the center.

5 With your sewing machine, sew your 1 ½" x 4 ½" rectangle to the left-hand side of your flower square.

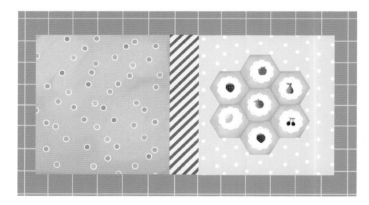

6 Then sew your 4 ½" square to the stripe fabric.

7 Iron on the 4 ½" x 9 ½" fusible interfacing to the wrong side of your completed front panel.

8 Add hand quilting detail around your hexagon flower.

9 Fold the pocket fabric in half lengthways, wrong sides together, and press.

10 Add a running stitch detail ¼" down from the fold line.

11 Lay the pocket onto the inside lining fabric along the bottom and baste stitch ⅛" from the edge into place.

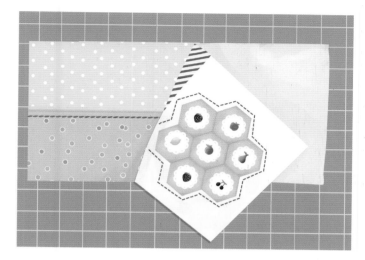

12 Face the front and inside panels right sides together and stitch ¼" seam around all the edges leaving a 2" turning gap at the back bottom right hand corner, remembering to backstitch at the start and end.

13 Turn right side out through the turning gap, press and slip stitch closed.

14 If you wish, embellish your felt pages or leave plain.

15 Fold your felt pages in half and pin at the fold. Center this fold in the middle of your needle book and with your sewing machine attach to your needle book.

16 Loop one end of the ribbon through the scissors, fold over and sew a button on to secure. At the other end, fold the ribbon and hand sew with a blind stitch to the inside of the needle book - see "Hand stitches" in the Techniques section.

PINCUSHION

1 Fussy cut and prepare 1" scallops x 9 (do not baste the bottoms), and lay your prepared scallops out in a pleasing manner. Then English Paper Piece them together along their straight sides.

2 Take your 3" x 11" low volume fabric to your ironing board. Fold in half lengthways and press. On the wrong side of your scallops apply a few small dots of appliqué glue to the fabric. Flip back over and align the top of the scallops with the pressed line. Allow the glue to dry and then appliqué your scallops down using a blind stitch.

Remove the papers.

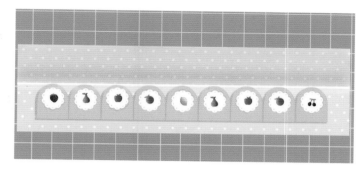

3 Iron the fusible interfacing to the back of the panel and add a running stitch along the top of the scallops.

4 Trim your panel back to 2" x 10". Sew the short ends together and set aside.

5 Place your two 2 ½" by 4" rectangles right sides together and with a 1" seam allowance sew 1" down. Leave a 2" turning gap and then sew the remaining 1", back stitching at the start and end of each seam. Press the seam allowance open.

6 Using the "Pincushion Top" cardstock template, center it over the rectangle just made and cut out the circle.

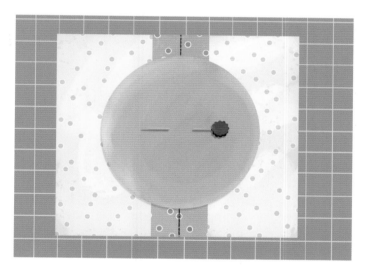

7 Take the ring that was made at step 4, fold it and mark the quarter marks with pins. Finger press the same quarter marks on the pincushion top. With right sides facing align these four points and pin.

Continue to pin your pincushion top to the sides.

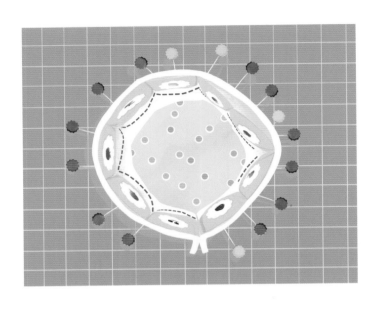

8 With your sewing machine, sew around the circle with a ¼" seam allowance, removing the pins as you go.

9 Fold and mark the quarter marks on the bottom, this time with pins. Finger press the same quarter marks on the Pincushion bottom. With right sides facing align these four points and pin. Again with your sewing machine, sew around the circle with a ¼" seam allowance, just like step 9, removing the pins as you go.

10 Turn right sides out, stuff with your desired filling and whip stitch closed.

SPRING TIME JOURNAL COVER

A perfect way to showcase a special illustration or a treasured piece of fabric.

FINISHED MEASUREMENTS
Closed
Approximately 8 ½" x 6 ¾"
Open
Approximately 8 ¾" x 11 ½"

SHAPES REQUIRED

▶ 1" hexagon x 90

FABRIC REQUIREMENTS

▶ Various fabrics for fussy cutting the hexagons
▶ 9 ¼" x 12" inside lining (a) *
▶ 6" x 9 ¼" inside cover (b) *
▶ 6" x 8" pocket (c) *
▶ 1 ¼" x 9 ¼" back cover binding (d) *
▶ A piece of parlan and white fabric the size of your English Paper Pieced panel.
▶ A5 notebook
▶ Illustration – optional

*This pattern can be adapted to fit any size journal/notebook by adjusting the size of your pieced panel, pockets etc. See step 5 for more information.

1 Cut and prepare 1" hexagons x 90 - see "Fussy cutting" and "Glue basting" in the Techniques section.

If you are making a cover for a larger journal, then you need to cut and prepare enough 1" hexagons to make a panel larger than the open surface dimensions of your journal. Quilting will also cause your panel to 'shrink' in size so be sure to make sure your panel is larger than needed.

Piece your panel - see "Joining your pieces" in the Techniques section.

2 Once you have pieced your panel make a quilt sandwich by fusing a piece of parlan to the back, and then use a piece of white fabric for the backing. Quilt as desired - see Refer to "Quilting" in the Techniques Section. Trim your panel to 12 ¼" x 17 ½".

3 Take the 6" x 8" pocket fabric (c) and fold it in half to create a 6" x 4" panel.

Top stitch across the fold with your sewing machine. Lay this on top of the 6" x 9 ¼" rectangle (b), pin to hold. On the right-hand side, fold the edge under ¼", iron and repeat. Using your sewing machine, top stitch down the length of the fold.

4 Lay your pieced panel right side up and then position the pocket panel right side down on the right-hand side of your pieced panel. With your sewing machine, sew the right hand seam, joining the two pieces. When folded over, this will create your pocket inside the front cover.

5 Trim your panel height to be ¾" taller than the journal/notebook you are covering. Mine is trimmed to 9 ¼" in height. This will be the height of your pieces (a), (b) and (d) if making a cover for a different sized journal.

6 Because every journal/notebook is a different thickness, do the following to make a cover that fits your journal perfectly. Slip the front cover of the journal under the pocket. Holding in place, close your journal. Tuck the back cover inside the back of the journal.

7 Carefully remove your journal, ensuring that the fold remains, and press the fold with your iron.

8 Take the back cover binding strip (d), fold over one long edge ¼" and press. Lay your cover right side down, position the binding strip as pictured and sew the raw edge side to the back of the pieced cover, right side facing the back as pictured.

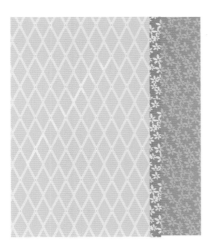

9 Fold over to the right side of the pieced panel and, with your sewing machine, top stitch into place.

10 If you are embellishing your journal cover, it is time to do it now. Position your embellishment and stitch into place as per your preferred method. I used a single strand of DMC thread color no. 951 and a running stitch – see "Hand stitches" in the Techniques section.

11 Lay your journal cover right side up and fold in the two sides of the cover and pin into place

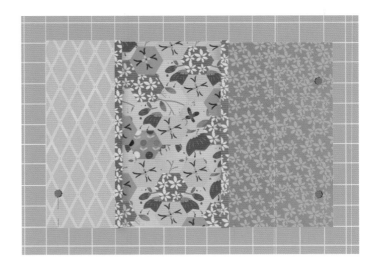

12 Take the 9 ¼" x 12" internal lining (a). Fold each 9 ¼" length over ¼" press, fold another ¼" press again and top stitch the folds down. Lay it right side down over the journal cover, centered as pictured.

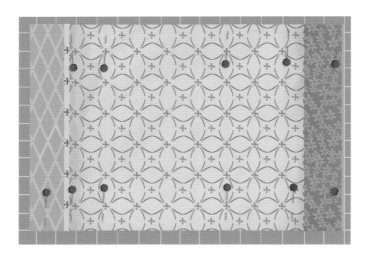

13 With your sewing machine, sew the top and bottom seam all the way cross, removing your pins as you go. Carefully trim the corners to remove any bulk when turned in the right way.

14 Turn right side out, and press with your iron. Insert your journal and you have finished. Your journal cover should be nice and snug when closed.

LINEN AND LACE FUSSY CUT PINCUSHIONS

Ooh la la! These pretty pincushions allow
you to explore fussy cutting on a small scale
and achieve beautiful results.

FINISHED MEASUREMENTS
Approximately 3 ½" x 4"

SHAPES REQUIRED

PINCUSHION 1

- 1" 6-point star x 12
- 2" hexagon x 1
- 1" x 2" rectangle x 6

PINCUSHION 2

- 1" 6-point star x 12
- 1" Hexagon x 6

FABRIC REQUIREMENTS

- 1 FQ for fussy cutting
- 5" x 11" piece of linen
- 5" square of solid pink
- 2 buttons
- Fibre fill

Using your fussy cutting mirror and your perspex templates have a play and explore all your fussy cutting options from your chosen fabrics – see "Fussy cutting" in the Techniques section.

PINCUSHION ONE

1 Cut and prepare :
- 1" fussy cut 6-point stars x 12
- 2" linen hexagon x 1
- 1" x 2" linen rectangles x 6
See "Glue basting" in the Techniques section.

2 Begin to piece your center star pieces - see "Joining your pieces" in the Techniques section.

3 Sew your remaining pieces to the outside of your star and then press with a warm iron. This is your pincushion top.

4 Attach the long sides of the rectangles to the sides of your pincushion top and then sew the short sides together making your pincushion appear wrong side out.

5 Remove your papers from your 12 star pieces only.

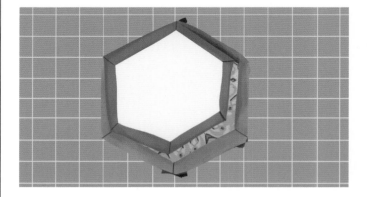

6 Begin to sew your base on ensuring right sides are facing.

TIP: For this pincushion I left my papers in the sides and base to maintain shape. This is optional. If you are choosing to do this, sew three sides of your hexagon to the side rectangles and carefully turn right side out. Sew two more sides to your hexagon base and proceed to Step 10 without removing your papers.

110

7 Leave two sides open. Remove your papers from the rectangles that have been sewn to your hexagon.

8 Carefully turn right sides out.

9 Stitch one more side to your base and remove your papers.

10 Fill your pincushion with your preferred filling. I have used Fibrefill.

11 Stitch closed.

PINCUSHION TWO

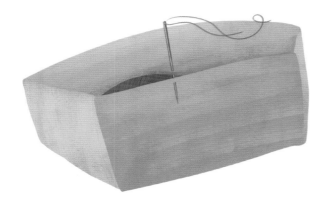

1 Cut and prepare:
- 1" fussy cut 6-point stars x 6
- 1" solid pink 6-point star x 6
- 1" hexagon x 6
See "Glue basting" in the Techniques section.
Make both your fussy cut star and your solid pink star.

2 Sew your hexagons to your fussy cut star as pictured and then sew your solid pink star to one of the hexagons.

3 Working in sections, sew the two sides of the hexagon together from point A to point B and then sew the star to the bottom from point B to point C.

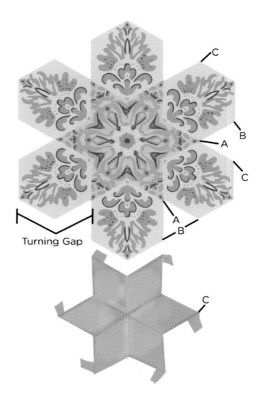

Turning Gap

4 Repeat all the way around in a circular motion, removing the papers as you go and leaving a turning gap at the end where shown. Your pincushion will begin to form a 'flat' ball. Carefully turn right sides out.

5 Fill your pincushion firmly with your preferred filling. I have used Fibrefill. Sew closed.

6 Sew through the middle of your pincushion using a long needle and double thread to attach a button to the top and bottom in the center, pulling firmly to create an indent to your pincushion. Tie off and you are finished.

PLACEMATS

There is nothing more perfect than a table set with handmade placements for a lazy Sunday afternoon ice-cream treat.

FINISHED MEASUREMENTS
Finished Size approximately 17 ¾" x 11 ¾"

SHAPES REQUIRED

▸ 1" hexagon x 33

FABRIC REQUIREMENTS

For 1 placement:

▸ Various fabrics for fussy cutting the hexagons
▸ 10" x 14" linen
▸ 4" x 5 ½" linen
▸ 4" x 12" pocket fabric

EPP panels:

▸ 2 ½" x 14" – panel (a) x 1
▸ 4" x 7" – panel (b) x 1
▸ 70" binding
▸ 19" x 14" batting/parlan
▸ 19" x 14" backing fabric

1 Cut and prepare : 1" hexagons x 33
See "Fussy cutting" and "Glue basting" in the Techniques section.

2 Piece two English Paper Piecing panels as pictured. See "Joining your pieces" in the Techniques section.

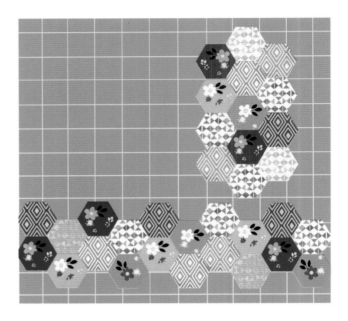

3 Remove your papers and unfold your seam allowance. Press with your iron.

4 Using your quilting ruler and your rotary cutter, trim your panels to:
2 ½" x 14" rectangle – panel (a)
4" x 7" rectangle – panel (b)

TIP: I left this panel a little longer so I didn't cut my hand sewing, thus eliminating the need to machine stitch around the panel as per the "Including EPP in any project" instructions in the Techniques section.

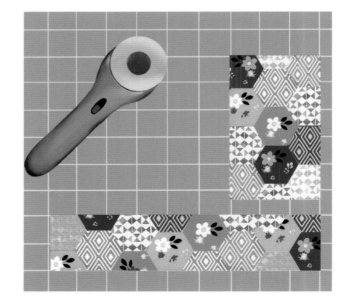

5 With your sewing machine, sew your 10" x 14" linen rectangle to the top of your EPP panel (a) and sew your 4" x 5 ½" linen rectangle to the bottom of your EPP panel (b).

6 Take your 4" x 12" pocket fabric and fold in half, wrong sides together to make a panel measuring 4" x 6" and press with your iron. Top stitch ¼" down from the fold.

7 Lay your large panel right sides up and then lay your pocket on the bottom right hand corner. Position your side panel right sides down along the right hand edge (over the pocket). Pin into place.

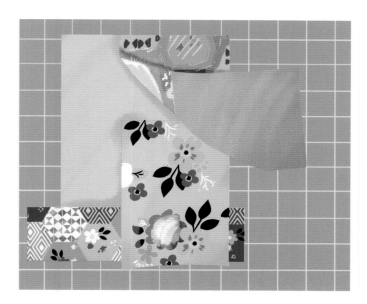

8 With your sewing machine, sew all the layers together. Trim off the overhang from step 4 now with your rotary cutter and ruler.

9 Open and press with your iron.

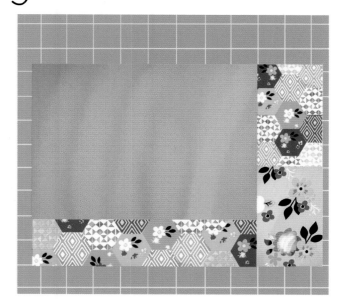

10 Make your quilt sandwich – see "Quilting" in the Techniques section.

11 Quilt in your desired method. I have "Quilted in the ditch" on my hexagon panels.

NOTE: Your hexagon panel sits lower than your pocket, so finish quilting this section and then flip the pocket over to the right and baste the pocket into place with your sewing machine, using a long basting stitch to hold it neatly in place.

12 Trim away the excess batting and backing fabric. Prepare and attach your binding – see "Binding" in the Techniques section.

HEXAGON CLOCK

My little girl loves handmade and this Hexagon Clock is the perfect addition to her bedroom. It is a fun way to show off some of your favourite prints or colors to brighten any room.

FINISHED MEASUREMENTS
Approximately 17 ¾" diameter

SHAPE REQUIRED

▶ 2" hexagon x 19

FABRIC REQUIREMENTS

▶ Various 4 ½" square scraps to make 19 hexagons.

OTHER REQUIREMENTS

▶ Clock mechanism
▶ Clock hands
▶ 1 sheet of white foam core board – minimum 17" x 18"
▶ Exacto knife
▶ Craft glue
▶ Wooden skewer (used for cooking)

1 Fussy cut and prepare - 2" hexagons x 19
See "Fussy cutting" and "Glue basting" in the Techniques section.

2 Lay your hexagons out in a pleasing manner and English Paper Piece your Hexagons together to form your shape. Refer to "Joining your Pieces" in the Techniques section but this time leave you papers in. DO NOT remove them for this project.

3 Press lightly with a warm iron to remove any folds in the papers. If any of your papers have come out, glue them back into place.

4 Lay your pieced panel on your foam core board and with a pencil trace around the outside being careful not to mark your fabrics. Small appliqué pins can be used to hold your EPP panel in place whilst you trace.

5 Carefully cut approximately ⅛" inside the drawn line with an exacto knife and ruler.

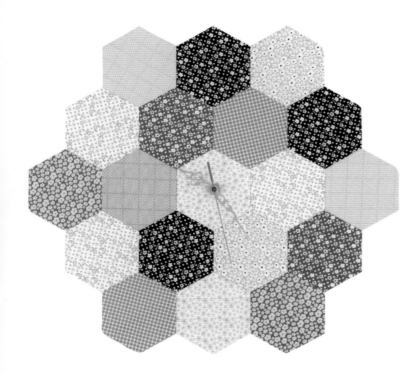

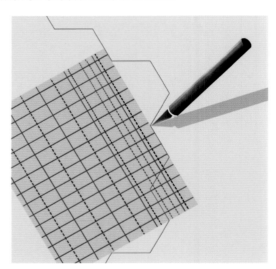

6 With your craft glue, glue your pieced panel to the foam core board, centering the panel over the board. Do not place any glue on the hexagon in the center that your clock mechanism with be mounted through. Allow the glue to dry. Binding clips are handy to place around the outside to hold in place whilst the glue dries.

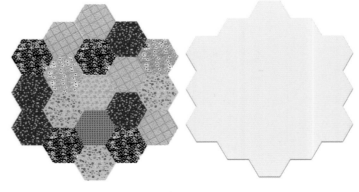

7 Very carefully, with your exacto knife, start to cut a small hole through the fabric, paper and foam core board. Slowly make the hole a little bigger so it fits the clock mechanism. You want a a nice firm fit. A wooden skewer can be used to help make the hole bigger in the foam core board.

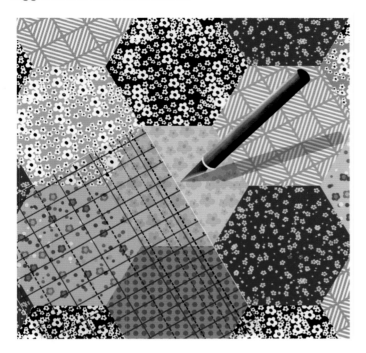

8 Mount your clock mechanism to the back and attach the clock hands as per the manufacturer's instructions.

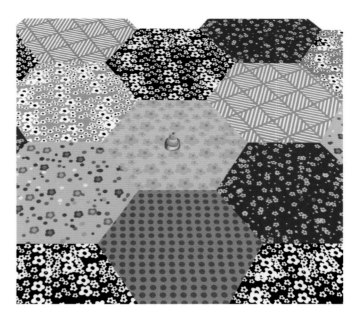

Mount to your wall and enjoy.

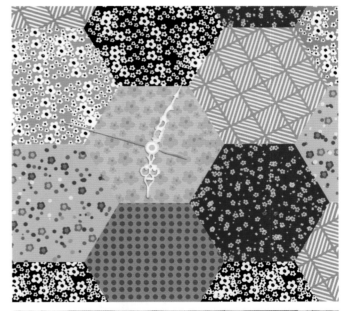

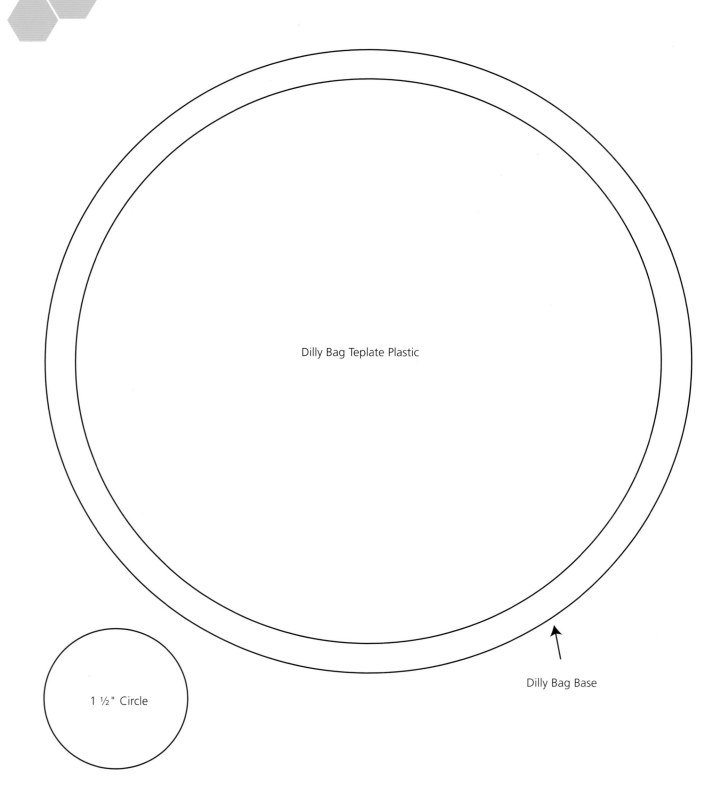

Dilly Bag Teplate Plastic

Dilly Bag Base

1 ½" Circle

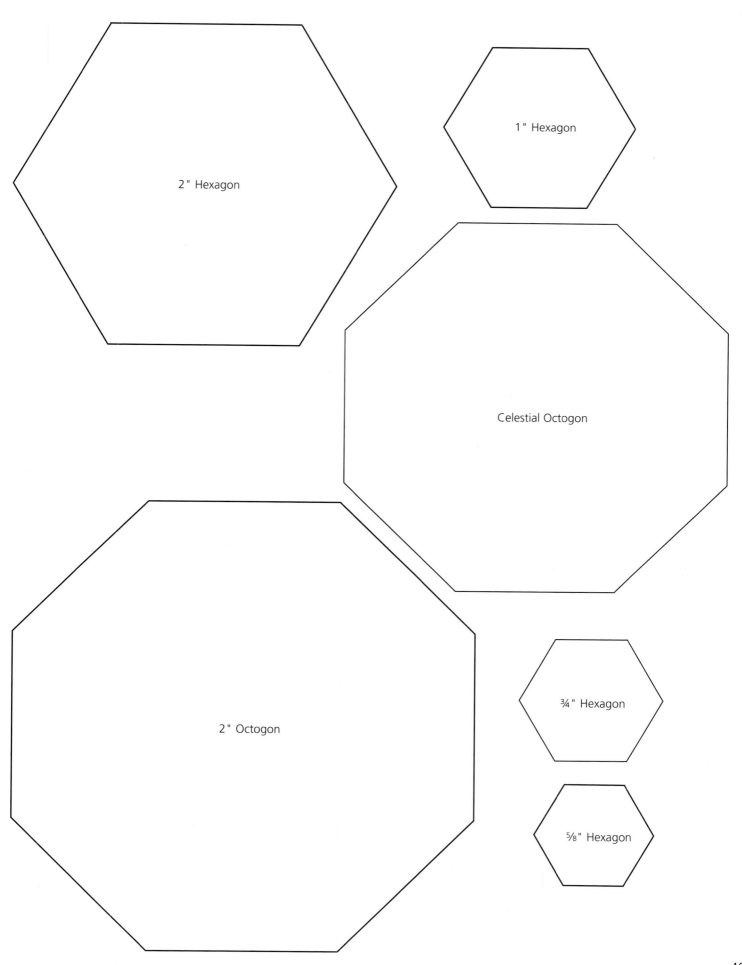

2" Hexagon

1" Hexagon

Celestial Octogon

2" Octogon

¾" Hexagon

⅝" Hexagon

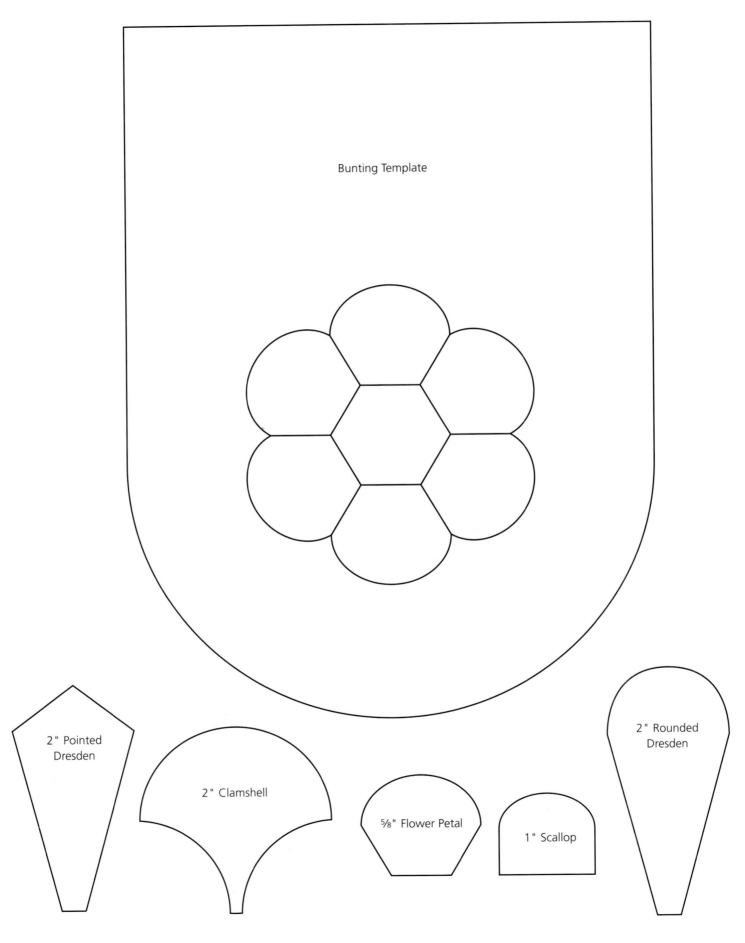

Bunting Template

2" Pointed Dresden

2" Clamshell

⅝" Flower Petal

1" Scallop

2" Rounded Dresden

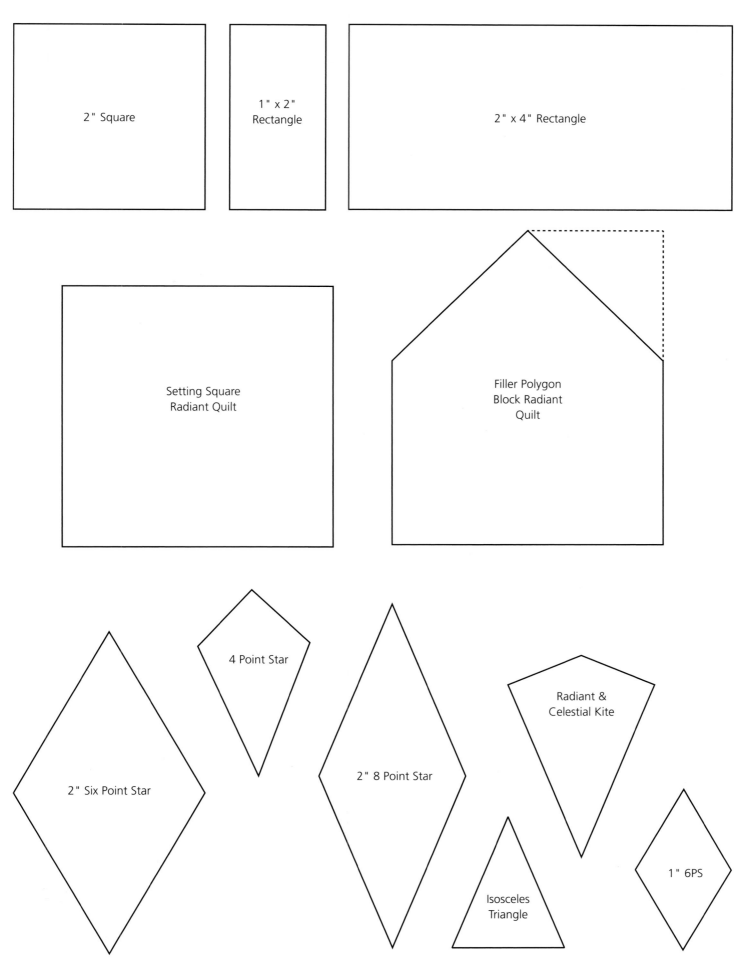

2" Square

1" x 2" Rectangle

2" x 4" Rectangle

Setting Square
Radiant Quilt

Filler Polygon
Block Radiant
Quilt

4 Point Star

2" Six Point Star

2" 8 Point Star

Radiant &
Celestial Kite

Isosceles
Triangle

1" 6PS

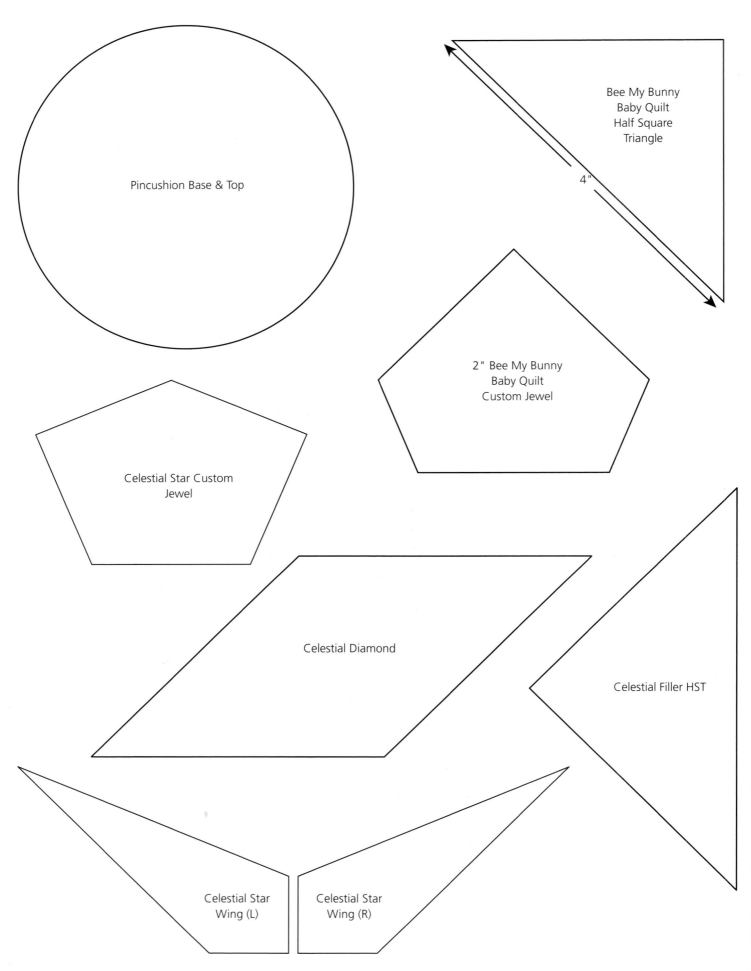

Pincushion Base & Top

Bee My Bunny
Baby Quilt
Half Square
Triangle

4"

2" Bee My Bunny
Baby Quilt
Custom Jewel

Celestial Star Custom
Jewel

Celestial Diamond

Celestial Filler HST

Celestial Star
Wing (L)

Celestial Star
Wing (R)

RESOURCES AND ACKNOWLEDGEMENTS

I love choosing fabrics for a new project. There really is something special about finding that perfect fabric. Here are some of the places that I love to visit and did visit for the special projects within my book and of course, additions to my stash.

AVA AND NEVE

For all my Liberty fabric needs I always turn to Ava and Neve. A wonderful Australian shop full of Liberty fabrics, supplies and notions. www.avaandneve.com.au

MINISTRY OF FABRIC

When looking for beautiful florals, chambrays and linens I always visit Alisha at Ministry of Fabric. www.ministryoffabric.com.au

FABRIC PIXIE

Always stocking fun, fresh and modern fabrics and trims. www.fabricpixie.com.au

THANK YOU

To Riley Blake Designs Australian Distributor Millhouse Collections for contributing fabric for several projects.

Special thank you to Michelle Palmer for the journal cover illustration. Michelle's original Illustrations can be found on ETSY by searching 'Michelle Palmer'.

LONG ARM QUILTER

For my long arm quilting I like to use and recommend Linda Cotton at Ladybug Quilting here in Bendigo, Australia.

Linda has quilted the following projects within my book, Raidiant, Be My Bunny Baby Quilt and Celestial Star.

A SPECIAL THANK YOU

To my family, thank you, you mean the world to me and without your support and unconditional love none of this would be possible. To my children, Aiden, Declyn, Keegan and Lily, "If your dreams do not scare you, you are not dreaming big enough". Dream big and aim high. Love, Mum xx

Please check www.lilabellelanecreations.com for availability and stockists of template and papers kits for patterns within this book.